NAVAL POSTGRADUATE SCHOOL
Monterey, California

THESIS

MARITIME IRREGULAR WARFARE: A LONG-RANGE VIEW

by

William R. Sutton

September 2000

Thesis Advisor:	John Arquilla
Second Reader:	Gordon H. McCormick

Approved for public release; distribution is unlimited.

REPORT DOCUMENTATION PAGE

Form Approved
OMB No. 0704-0188

Public reporting burden for this collection of information is estimated to average 1 hour per response, including the time for reviewing instruction, searching existing data sources, gathering and maintaining the data needed, and completing and reviewing the collection of information. Send comments regarding this burden estimate or any other aspect of this collection of information, including suggestions for reducing this burden, to Washington headquarters Services, Directorate for Information Operations and Reports, 1215 Jefferson Davis Highway, Suite 1204, Arlington, VA 22202-4302, and to the Office of Management and Budget, Paperwork Reduction Project (0704-0188) Washington DC 20503.

1. AGENCY USE ONLY *(Leave blank)*	2. REPORT DATE September 2000	3. REPORT TYPE AND DATES COVERED Master's Thesis
4. TITLE AND SUBTITLE Maritime Irregular Warfare: A Long-Range View		5. FUNDING NUMBERS
6. AUTHOR(S) Sutton, William R.		
7. PERFORMING ORGANIZATION NAME(S) AND ADDRESS(ES) Naval Postgraduate School Monterey, CA 93943-5000		8. PERFORMING ORGANIZATION REPORT NUMBER
SPONSORING / MONITORING AGENCY NAME(S) AND ADDRESS(ES) N/A		10. SPONSORING / MONITORING AGENCY REPORT NUMBER

SUPPLEMENTARY NOTES The views expressed in this thesis are those of the author and do not reflect the official policy or position of the Department of Defense or the U.S. Government.

12a. DISTRIBUTION / AVAILABILITY STATEMENT Approved for public release; distribution is unlimited.	12b. DISTRIBUTION CODE

ABSTRACT *(maximum 200 words)*

Maritime irregular warfare (MIW) has been around since the dawn of sea power. While conventional naval warfare holds the premier position in naval affairs, MIW constitutes a less understood but equally important "other" tradition that merits closer attention. History demonstrates a link between the evolution of regular naval warfare and its irregular counterpart. When fully understood and correctly utilized, MIW actions have proven extremely effective at providing unconventional solutions to complex military problems. Consistently, MIW forces have powerfully affected the outcomes of conflict both at sea and on land. Through the skillful employment of MIW, this long historical pattern can continue to affect conflicts of the 21st century.

In an era of rapid change, the ability to clearly identify and understand emerging trends in conflict and military affairs is an essential element in assessing MIW's future. As conventional warfare begins to realign for future threats, practitioners of MIW need to begin thinking proactively about how MIW can stay relevant, and the concerted actions that need to be taken in order to fit into the future of warfare. This thesis is an attempt to take a first glimpse of MIW's future.

14. SUBJECT TERMS Maritime Irregular Warfare, Information Age Conflict		15. NUMBER OF PAGES 120
		16. PRICE CODE
17. SECURITY CLASSIFICATION OF REPORT Unclassified	18. SECURITY CLASSIFICATION OF THIS PAGE Unclassified	19. SECURITY CLASSIFI- CATION OF ABSTRACT Unclassified

20. LIMITATION OF ABSTRACT UL

THIS PAGE INTENTIONALLY LEFT BLANK

MARITIME IRREGULAR WARFARE: A LONG-RANGE VIEW

William R. Sutton
Lieutenant, United States Navy
B.S., Naval Postgraduate School, 2000

Submitted in partial fulfillment of the
requirements for the degree of

MASTER OF SCIENCE IN DEFENSE ANALYSIS

from the

NAVAL POSTGRADUATE SCHOOL
September 2000

Author: _____
William R. Sutton

Approved by: _____
John Arquilla, Thesis Advisor

_____
Gordon H. McCormick, Second Reader

_____
Gordon H. McCormick, Chairman
Special Operations Academic Group

THIS PAGE INTENTIONALLY LEFT BLANK

ABSTRACT

Maritime irregular warfare (MIW) has been around since the dawn of sea power. While conventional naval warfare holds the premier position in naval affairs, MIW constitutes a less understood but equally important "other" tradition that merits closer attention. History demonstrates a link between the evolution of regular naval warfare and its irregular counterpart. When fully understood and correctly utilized, MIW actions have proven extremely effective at providing unconventional solutions to complex military problems. Consistently, MIW forces have powerfully affected the outcomes of conflict both at sea and on land. Through the skillful employment of MIW, this long historical pattern can continue to affect the conflicts of the 21st century.

In an era of rapid change, the ability to clearly identify and understand emerging trends in conflict and military affairs is an essential element in assessing MIW's future. As conventional warfare begins to realign for future threats, practitioners of MIW need to begin thinking proactively about how MIW can stay relevant, and the concerted actions that need to be taken in order to fit into the future of warfare. This thesis is an attempt to take a first glimpse of MIW's future.

THIS PAGE INTENTIONALLY LEFT BLANK

TABLE OF CONTENTS

I. INTRODUCTION...1

  A. METHODOLOGY...2

II. THE EVOLUTION OF MARITIME IRREGULAR WARFARE 5

  A. THE MARITIME IRREGULAR WARFARE TYPOLOGY 7

  B. CURRENT TRENDS IN MARITIME IRREGULAR WARFARE............................26

    1. *Mastering the Sea, Air, and Land*...28

      a) Multi-Medium Capabilities 28

      b) Hybrid Platforms...30

  C. LINKING THE REGULAR AND IRREGULAR APPROACH...............................34

III. INFORMATION AGE CONFLICT...41

  A. THE NATURE OF THE BEAST..41

  B. BACKGROUND AND BASIC APPROACH 42

  C. THE EMERGING GEOSTRATEGIC SETTING..45

    1. *The Geostrategic Reordering*..47

    2. *The Rapid Pace of Technological Change* 51

  D. THE REVOLUTION IN MILITARY AFFAIRS...55

    1. *The RMA as a Concept*..56

    2. *A Two-tiered Approach to the RMA*...58

      a) The Near-Term Phase..58

      b) The Long-Term Phase..60

    3. *The Trends in Military Affairs*..61

      a) The High-technology Trends...62

      b) The Highly-sophisticated Trends....................................65

E.   TACTICAL TECHNOLOGY TRENDS 68

F.   INTERPRETING THE EVOLUTIONARY FRAMEWORK 73

IV.   **IMPLICATIONS FOR THE FUTURE** 77

A.   STAYING POWER 77

B.   HIGH-LEVERAGE FORCES 84

C.   INTEGRATED AND INDEPENDENT MARITIME IRREGULAR WARFARE 89

        1.   *Decisive Action* 94

        2.   *The MIW Campaign* 96

LIST OF REFERENCES 101

INITIAL DISTRIBUTION LIST 105

I. INTRODUCTION

Maritime irregular warfare (MIW) has been around since the dawn of sea power. While conventional naval warfare holds the premier position in naval affairs, MIW constitutes a less understood but equally important "other" tradition in naval affairs that merits closer attention. History demonstrates a link between the evolution and rise of regular naval warfare and its irregular counterpart. When fully understood and correctly utilized, MIW actions have proven extremely effective at providing unconventional solutions to complex military problems. Consistently, MIW forces have powerfully affected the outcomes of conflict both at sea and on land. Through the skillful employment of MIW, this long historical pattern can continue to affect conflicts of the 21st century.

In an era of rapid change, the ability to clearly identify and understand emerging trends in conflict and military affairs is an essential element in assessing MIW's future. New types of crises, coupled with rapid technological change, have combined to produce an increasingly complex geostrategic operating environment. As conventional warfare begins to realign for future threats, practitioners of MIW will need to begin thinking proactively about how MIW can stay relevant, and the concerted actions that need to be taken in order to fit into the future of warfare. This thesis is an attempt to take a first glimpse of MIW's future.

This thesis will first identify and examine the MIW concept, then analyze the recent developments in military affairs. The working hypothesis is that, together, these two areas hold the key to understanding MIW's future. To this end, the arguments advanced will help develop a better understanding of the critical environmental factors and dynamic relationships that have combined to define MIW's past, and will ultimately shape its future.

A.   METHODOLOGY

This thesis begins by examining the MIW concept, and outlining the critical components that lie at its core. Due to MIW's changing practices over time, a usable definition can only be reached by building an accurate typology of MIW, illustrated by brief historical case descriptions that best identify and explain the maritime irregular warfare phenomenon. The purpose of the examples included in the typology will be to show the range and versatility of the

MIW concept and its progression through time. Along with the typology, an additional corollary hypothesis examining the interdependent relationship between the regular and irregular forms of naval warfare is included to further refine maritime irregular warfare conceptually. In addition, an overview of the current trends in MIW will be conducted in order to clarify its current global posture. At the conclusion of this chapter, the reader should be up to date and armed with a general understanding of what MIW is, where MIW came from, and MIW's current global prospects.

Following the capability chapter will be a look at developments in crisis, conflict, and war in the information age. The primary purpose of this is to build an analytical framework for understanding the future strategic environment and identifying the trends in military affairs. A majority of the themes and concepts developed in this chapter will come from existing literature and research pertaining to this subject. Therefore, this chapter will be organized to provide a condensed stocktaking of the most relevant concepts and themes consistently found throughout this body of work.

Finally, by combining the arguments made in the MIW concept section with the analysis of information age conflict, this thesis will provide an assessment of MIW's future. The conclusions this thesis advances are not meant to provide a detailed step-by-step roadmap to MIW's future. Instead, it is hoped that a conceptual, yet valid and usable view of MIW's future can be captured and projected as a future reference point to guide thinking and planning. In addition to putting the irregular side of naval warfare into perspective and offering a vision of MIW's future, it is hoped that the approach and broader themes developed throughout this thesis will spark increased interest in, and discussion of, the future of maritime irregular warfare.

II. THE EVOLUTION OF MARITIME IRREGULAR WARFARE

> Whosoever can hold the sea has command of everything.
>
> - *Themistocles (524-469 B.C.)*

The use of maritime irregular warfare in conflict is not a recent development. The irregular approach has been an integral part of naval warfare strategies ever since man has waged war upon or from the seas. Although these operations were not always conducted by, "specially organized, trained, and equipped military and paramilitary forces,"[1] because they did exist outside the sphere of accepted conventional naval operations at the time, these earlier cases do merit inclusion as MIW operations. Prior to the advent of the specially organized maritime irregular warfare forces we see employed today, many operations were, and in some cases still are, undertaken by regular forces conducting irregular missions outside the realm of conventional operations. It is in this context that we are able to see the emergence of the maritime irregular warfare concept. This approach to MIW facilitates a much broader interpretation of the irregular

---

[1] Joint Pub 1-02, *Department of Defense Dictionary of Military and Associated Terms*, 1 December 1989.

approach, and of MIW as a concept, allowing the true origins and evolutionary nature of MIW to be better studied. In trying to build an analytically useful typology to help explain MIW, this broader approach also helps capture the concept and true spirit of the irregular approach to naval warfare.

The primary goal of this section is to examine the advantages of the MIW concept and identify where MIW fits across the spectrum of naval warfare. Thus, this section is organized to recognize four distinct traits that, combined, help to explain maritime irregular warfare. To begin with, the MIW typology is structured to trace MIW's historical links and show the evolution of MIW through time. Second, the typology provides a review of some of the different forms MIW has taken throughout history. The third objective of the typology is to recognize MIW's ability to operate across different levels of war and along different time lines.[2] Finally, this thesis attempts to emphasize the key elements and traits that have historically characterized and shaped MIW operations.

---

[2] This has to do with MIW's ability to influence the operational and strategic levels of war, and to be utilized offensively or defensively for both short duration and protracted special operations.

The historical cases referenced in this section are not meant to be detailed case studies. Instead they are used illustratively to help build the typology and aid in the identification of MIW's central themes and essential elements. The cases presented are examples of both successful and failed MIW operations. Often, the success or failures of these types of operations hinge on factors that have nothing to do with the validity of the concept or approach. By their very nature, MIW operations carry a high degree of operational risk, and success in combat can never be guaranteed. Relying solely on success or failure criteria as a means of explaining the MIW concept limits gaining a more comprehensive understanding. The cases discussed in this chapter were chosen in order to develop the most complete picture of the MIW phenomenon.

A.   THE MARITIME IRREGULAR WARFARE TYPOLOGY

The origins of the maritime irregular warfare concept can be traced back to the classical period. Ancient maritime raiders, whether attacking shipping at sea or targets of opportunity ashore, represent the early beginnings of a form of MIW operations that would continue essentially unchanged well into the Middle Ages. It is in the ancient maritime raiding context that the first instances of the irregular approach at sea can be seen. A sample of the early approach to MIW is described here,

> The Periclean Strategy in the Peloponnesian War, for example, relied heavily upon a protracted special operations campaign of pinprick raids against the Spartans and their allies. Later on, after the fall of the Roman Empire, the Vikings would raise raiding to a science, and incorporate also some elements of "persisting," as their occupations of Normandy and Sicily, and settlement of Russia, attest. Perhaps the most sustained raiding occurred, though, in the long twilight struggle between Islam and Christendom in the Mediterranean. For centuries, both parties preyed on the shipping of the other, sometimes sparking larger conflicts, as in Suleiman's costly (and unsuccessful) mid-16th century invasion of Malta...[3]

In this excerpt we can plainly see the ancient beginnings and early successes of the irregular approach to naval warfare. This passage also contains the threads of several other MIW-specific elements worth mentioning. First, is the compelling fact that naval guerrillas have been able to leverage the advantages of an indirect approach throughout the classical period, suggesting that MIW has long been a fundamental part of naval strategy. This, supported later by the proposition that a rise in conventional naval warfare leads directly to a rise in unconventional warfare, is an essential point providing the

---

[3] John Arquilla, ed., *From Troy to Entebbe: Special Operations in Ancient and Modern Times* (Lanham MD: University Press of America, 1996), 11.

foundation upon which the MIW concept is built. This quote also highlights the fact that MIW's ancient beginnings were not confined to one particular area or group. Where there was combat on the water, inevitably there was an element of unconventional warfare in some form in order to complement and complete classical maritime strategies. Although the general form MIW took remained relatively consistent throughout this time period, the advantages of the irregular approach and the opportunities it afforded naval warfare strategists were already beginning to be thoroughly explored and tested as far back as the classical period.

MIW took a major evolutionary step forward in the late 1500's when Sir Francis Drake unleashed a new form of maritime raiding that changed the naval balance by refining and honing the tactics employed by earlier naval guerrillas. Drake's impact was significant,

> He was a master mariner and naval strategist who took full advantage of the marriage of gun and sail that revolutionized sea power and led to the many voyages of discovery and conquest that made Europeans the masters of the world for so long. Yet he also exhibited a particular talent for amphibious raiding, and for leading irregular forces on land. The tradition of special operations that he began had a powerful influence on British strategic thought; and one can see, in such conflicts as the Seven Years' War (1756-1763), an almost Periclean approach to raiding as a means of wearing down the enemy.[4]

---

[4] *Ibid.*, 11-12.

Already a highly respected mariner and strategist, Drake was able to strike targets ashore by coupling the mobility provided by the sea with an effective amphibious capability incorporating the use of small land forces. Drake's constant pressure and ubiquitous presence allowed him to win a long series of impressive engagements in the Caribbean and along the coasts of mainland Europe. Drake's land and sea operations also brought with them a distinct psychological effect. For example when Drake's fleet was rumored to be operating in a particular area, one author noted that in response, "[t]he whole of the Caribbean area was by this time in a state of nervous hubbub in which the wildest rumours gained credence..."[5] Drake's modification of the generic *guerre de course*[6] strategy to include strategically important targets ashore is significant in the evolution of MIW over time. As an analysis of Drake's exploits in the Caribbean at the time suggests, "It [*Drake's fleet*] had been absent just ten months and it had achieved moral and political results out of all proportion to its

---

[5] *Ibid.*, 17.

[6] The French term *guerre de course* refers to the age-old strategy of using fast ships for coastal defense and commerce raiding.

material consequences."[7] By capitalizing on initiative, pertinent and time sensitive intelligence, and the strategic flexibility offered by his vision of the indirect approach, Drake was able to exploit opportunities for massive strategic, and economic, gain. In the process, his unique vision and unorthodox methods revolutionized sea power and his exploits had a lasting effect on British strategic thought.

In an interesting side note, it was Drake's grand vision and success that spawned future naval guerrillas like the notorious Capt. Morgan, who continued the marauding tradition and became one of history's most feared corsairs.

This indirect pattern of naval warfare persisted into modern times. For example, in World War I the British Royal Navy attempted several audacious strategic maritime special operations that continued the tradition pioneered by Drake. The two cases examined here were both in response to the effective German U-boat campaign slowly paralyzing British war production and sea communications. Together they show the range and versatility of the MIW concept in a more modern setting. The first example involves an examination of the Q-ship phenomenon described below.

---

[7] Arquilla, ed., *From Troy to Entebbe: Special Operations in Ancient and Modern Times*, 19.

These [*Q-ships*] were innocent-looking merchantmen manned by volunteer naval crews with a powerful but carefully concealed armament. In the past, merchantmen had often been painted to look like men o'war with dummy wooden guns. This ruse which saved many a ship from pirates or its country's enemies was effectively reversed in the Q-ship, which rapidly assumed a legendary wolf-in-sheep's-clothing reputation in the service. The formula for success with these vessels was to invite attack by proceeding alone in the danger areas. At least until 1917, the U-boat usually surfaced on sighting its intended victim and then, with or without warning, opened fire and sank the ship by gunfire, reserving torpedoes for special occasions and targets, like ocean liners and warships. On sighting a surfaced U-boat, a "panic party" would noisily take to the Q-ship's boat, perhaps complete with parrot cage, while the gun crews remained concealed awaiting their opportunity of giving the enemy a short, well-aimed, and fatal volley.[8]

Early Q-ship successes were encouraging, although their overall effectiveness as a submarine killer was never substantial, and diminished over time. The real strategic value, and overall effect, of this unique example of a maritime irregular warfare campaign is not found in terms of U-boat sinkings, but rather in the unintended consequences that followed the Q-ships' employment. The fear of Q-ship operations forced the *Kriegsmarine* to radically change its submarine doctrine away from surfaced attacks. In turn, this shift toward sinkings without warning made U-boats less

---

[8] Richard Hough, *The Great War at Sea 1914-1918* (Oxford University Press, 1983), 303-304.

effective because they ran out of torpedoes and had to return to base sooner, while at the same time angering certain neutrals, in particular the United States, which Germany could not afford to have an enemy.

Later in the war Britain again turned toward the advantages of MIW and the indirect approach in order to solve the German U-boat dilemma, except this time in the form of a strategic *coup de main*[9] targeting several maritime choke points. As conceived, the blocking of Zeebrugge was designed to avoid the U-boat's strengths at sea and in port, and instead attack an alternative weakness by putting a "cork" in the German U-boat bases stationed along the coast of Flanders.

The submarine base at Bruges, situated along the Flanders coast, afforded German U-boats operating against British shipping with an ideal offensive and defensive location. This proximity to the English Channel and the North Sea cut down on submarine transit time, allowing U-boats to spend more time on station attacking Allied targets. Defensively, the submarine pens at Bruges were equally formidable as this excerpt points out,

---

[9] *Coup de main* refers to operations that are characterized by swift, decisive action, and intended to yield strategic results.

There was no chance whatever of destroying the flotillas of U-boats and destroyers once they were inside their bases because they could simply fade away into the maze-like canals and channels inland. Bruges itself, eight miles from Zeebrugge with which it was linked by a ship canal, made a marvelous, virtually invulnerable, hide-out.[10]

In April 1918 the Royal Navy began preparations for an operation designed to take the U-boats stationed at Bruges out of the war by purposely sinking three blocking ships in the canal entrance located at Zeebrugge. The Zeebrugge operation was part of a much larger British effort to finally clear out the German wasps' nest in Flanders. These blocking ships would have the effect of cutting off German submarine access to the sea. In order to allow the blocking ships a reasonable chance of reaching the canal entrance, the British also decided to assault the heavily fortified mole, which guarded the entrance, with a relatively small landing force.

As planned, the operation would commence with a deceptive naval bombardment and smoke screen designed to allow the task force to approach the port facility. The mole would then be cutoff from reinforcements by purposely ramming two explosive laden submarines into the only rail viaduct connecting the mole to the mainland, and then

---

[10] Hough, *The Great War at Sea 1914-1918*, 315.

detonating them. Finally, three specially equipped surface craft were to be brought alongside the mole allowing naval commandos to disembark and assault the gun emplacements that threatened to sink the blocking ships prior to reaching their designated positions.

Although meticulously planned and rehearsed, the execution of this mission fell well short of the desired objective for several reasons. The wind patterns expected and needed in order to allow the assault force to approach the mole under smoke screen changed direction at the critical moment, leaving the British ships exposed to intense German shore fire. One of the two breaching submarines never arrived, although the second submarine did complete its mission by blowing a 100-foot gap in the viaduct. Under withering fire, the blockships were unable to sink themselves in their allotted positions. In the aftermath of the commando assault, which was the scene of some of the most brutal hand-to-hand fighting of the war, what was envisioned as a strategic *coup de main* provided only a mild inconvenience to the Germans.

The World War One examples of MIW are important because together they show the range and versatility of the MIW concept. The Q-ship phenomenon and the blocking of Zeebrugge sit at opposite ends of the MIW spectrum (Figure 1). One a protracted special operation waged against highly mobile targets at sea whose full effect could only be gauged over the long run. The other envisioned as a strategic *coup de main* against a fixed target ashore intended to reap immediate, decisive results. Both undertakings, although radically different in approach, possessed MIW's potential to shift the overall naval balance of the war with a small investment in men and materiel.

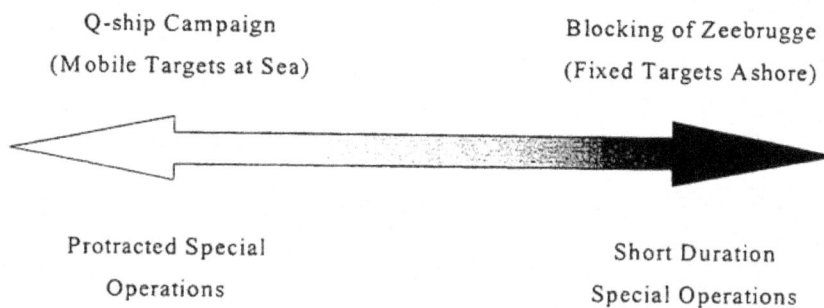

Q-ship Campaign   Blocking of Zeebrugge

(Mobile Targets at Sea)   (Fixed Targets Ashore)

Protracted Special   Short Duration

Operations   Special Operations

Figure 1. The Maritime Irregular Warfare Spectrum

There is no question that it took nerves of steel and a very "special" crew to man Britain's Q-ships. Perhaps just as important was the unconventional mindset that conceived of this plan and then allowed it to be put into action. Although the final numbers the Q-ships registered during the war were small, the consequences of this protracted special operation played a decisive role in the war's outcome by provoking U.S. entry into the war in response to Germany's unrestricted U-boat attacks, especially direct torpedo attack without surfacing. Britain's employment of Q-ships during World War I serves as a classic example of MIW providing a vital unconventional function that would yield long-term, strategic results.

In contrast to the subtlety of a protracted special operation, the blocking of Zeebrugge was launched with the intention of shifting the naval balance in a single decisive action. In the final analysis the blocking of Zeebrugge did not meet its intended objective. While the operation fell short of the desired result, undertaking the mission did provide Britain and the Royal Navy with sorely needed inspiration at a low point in the war. In addition, this bold naval action on Germany's flank succeeded in diverting attention, and German forces, away from the stagnant land campaign in France.

In recent times, maritime irregular warfare has continued to evolve alongside its conventional counterpart, as technological innovations allowed modern-day naval guerrillas to continue to exploit their maritime niche. For this reason, World War II provides the most comprehensive picture of the MIW concept in action and it's effect on conventional strategy.

In the Pacific campaign, motor torpedo (PT) boats originally designed to conduct stealthy hit-and-run torpedo attacks on enemy shipping at night radically transformed their mission by the end of the war as, "the need for shallow-draft vessels to operate offshore in support of the ground forces"[11] became apparent. Post-war analyses have called into question the PT's reputation as a big-ship killer and found that PT capabilities in main fleet action have been overstated and romanticized.[12] Two factors that weighed heavily during all PT attacks were the experience level of the crew and the record of the notoriously unreliable, World War I-vintage, Mk 8 torpedo. For the PT boat, experience, reliable torpedoes, and aggressiveness were the keys to successful night attacks on larger vessels. Unfortunately, getting all three in the same PT boat at the opportune moment was rare. Even so, the PT's unconventional methods did afford U.S. strategists with a rapid reaction and low-cost means of blunting the Imperial Japanese Navy's

---

[11] Curtis Nelson, *Hunters in the Shallows: A History of the PT Boat* (Dulles VA: Brassey's, 1998), 163.

[12] William White, *They Were Expendable* (Naval Institute Press, 1998), is one book that overstates the PT's torpedo attack capability.

conventional advantage early in the Pacific campaign as this excerpt points out,

> Though the PT's torpedo potency left much to be desired, they often succeeded, by the threat of their shadowy presence and the aggressiveness of their attacks, in "rendering the transport of supplies exceptionally difficult" and giving the Japanese ships "many a bitter pill to swallow."[13]

There is no doubt that the PT's were specialized weapons requiring specialized training and crews. Operating in small formations from isolated island bases, the nocturnal PT's proved far more effective later on in their "barge-busting" role against near shore Japanese logistical lines than in their originally conceived torpedo-throwing role. Toward the end of the war PT's were a well-integrated part of the U.S. strategy in the Pacific. The Allied response to Japanese near shore logistical traffic came in the form of a dynamic one-two punch, with PT's operating at night and aircraft intercepting barge traffic during the day. In addition these "mosquito boats" offered commanders a unique and unequaled flexibility by, "Transporting troops, landing secret reconnaissance patrols, and performing other close-support duties for land forces..."[14] The versatility

---

[13] Nelson, *Hunters in the Shallows: A History of the PT Boat*, 161.

[14] *Ibid.*, 168.

of this small unit and its ability to evolve over time allowed the PT's to better serve the needs of the Fleet by affecting conflict at sea, in its limited torpedo boat role, and ashore, in its more effective attacks on Japanese supply lines. A realistic assessment of the PT's value after the war reveals that,

> ...the PT's hull and engines gave the Allies a readily available, mass-producible, seaworthy, fast, maneuverable, shallow-draft gun platform for dealing with Japanese coast-hugging logistical traffic...Because of them the United States Navy built not just a torpedo boat or a gunboat, but one superbly versatile man-of-war.[15]

Meanwhile, in the Mediterranean Theater, the Italian 10th Light Flotilla (*Decima Mas/Mariassalto*) built a MIW organization that represented the cutting edge of unconventional naval warfare at the time. By utilizing a wide variety of platforms and capabilities during the war, *Decima Mas* was able to contest the Allies conventional superiority in the Mediterranean. Geography seems to have played a role in why the Italians turned to unconventional maritime attacks, "From the Italian perspective, their Navy was sandwiched between the British Mediterranean Fleet at Alexandria and the French Fleet at Toulon together with such British forces as could be deployed from the Atlantic

---

[15] *Ibid.*, 206-207.

Fleet."[16] In response to this situation the Italians required a capability that could cheaply and quickly reduce the number of units ranged against them. MIW provided the Italians with a solution that over time would become the sole offensive arm of the Royal Italian Navy (RMI/*Regia Marina*).

In order to meet the challenge, the Italians experimented with a wide variety of MIW concepts and became particularly effective in their use of combat swimmers and human torpedoes[17] to attack ships at anchor. The emphasis the Italians placed on these types of operations can be seen in the sophistication of their organization. The *Decima Mas* was organized into two distinct parts, ". . .a surface group and a sub-surface weapons group. The former dealt with the operation of the fast explosive motor boats and the latter

---

[16] Paul Kemp, *Underwater Warriors* (Annapolis MD: The Naval Institute Press, 1996), 23.

[17] Human torpedo refers to the "wet" two-man *Maiale (Siluro a Lenta Corsa)* mini-submarine. The *Maiale* was similar in size and shape to a conventional torpedo. The two-man crew sat astride the craft with closed circuit dive gear and the forward operator controlling the direction and ballast of the craft with a joystick. At a speed of 4.5 knots the *Maiale* had a range of 4 miles and at 2.3 knots a range of 15 miles. Upon reaching a target, the operators would remove and attach the 220kg-300kg warhead located at the front of the craft, then exfiltrate the target area with their submersible.

with human torpedoes and assault frogmen."[18] Both groups were effective during the war. Although the groups were separate and could conduct operations independently, as with the successful human torpedo attack on Alexandria in December 1941, they could also be quickly reconstituted for combined attacks, as witnessed during the ill-fated surface and sub-surface attack on Malta in July 1941.

In addition to the 10th Light Flotilla's advanced organizational structure was an equally impressive support component. For transiting to and from targets, the Italians quickly adopted the practice of using specially configured conventional submarines. Pressure-tight containers attached to the submarine's casing allowed Italian frogmen to transport their human torpedoes and MTB[19] boats without being exposed to the elements. Initially, on arriving at a pre-arranged drop-off point, the submarine would surface and the naval commandos would quickly remove and launch their assault craft. Later, the Italians developed an entry/exit method that allowed them to launch and recover while the

---

[18] Kemp, *Underwater Warriors*, 24.

[19] The 10th Light Flotilla utilized several different configurations of Motor Touring (*Motorscafo Turismo*) boats (MTB). These were high-speed platforms, 30-33kts, with a crew of 1-2 men designed to attack ships by launching torpedoes, or impacting and then detonating on contact.

submarine remained submerged, greatly reducing the submarine's vulnerability.

Along with highly trained personnel and specially designed submarines, the 10th Light Flotilla also employed specially configured surface vessels to act as "mothercraft" for launching and recovering from missions. As an example of the Italians level of sophistication, for attacks on the British Fleet anchored at Gibraltar, the 10th Light Flotilla launched *Gamma* assault frogmen[20] and *Maiale* operations from a derelict Italian tanker, the *Olterra*, laying close by at Algeciras. Scuttled by its Italian crew at the outbreak of the war, the *Olterra* was refloated by the neutral Spanish, and subtly remanned by a detachment from the *Decima Mas*. The *Olterra*, because of its proximity to Gibraltar, served as an ideal staging base for attacks on the British Fleet. The *Decima Mas* detachment reconfigured the *Olterra* into a floating support base complete with all the tools necessary to maintain several human torpedoes and a submerged trapdoor for launching and recovering frogmen unobserved.

---

[20] *Gamma* assault frogmen, or combat swimmers, were equipped with Belloni dive suits and closed circuit breathing apparatus. Their primary mission was to penetrate harbors undetected and then attach limpet mines to enemy ships in port.

The balanced and integrated approach used by the Italians offers a modern look at MIW's full potential. By bringing together MTB high speed surface attacks, *Gamma* assault frogmen, wet and dry mini-submarines, and the appropriate conventional craft to support these operations, the Italians were able to deploy a potent unconventional response to the Allies conventional superiority in the Mediterranean. The 10th Light Flotilla also continued to push the boundaries of MIW by innovating radically new techniques and capitalizing on cutting edge technologies. By the end of the war the *Decima Mas* record was impressive, "in under three years of warfare, the Decima Mas was responsible for sinking or damaging four warships and twenty-seven merchant ships totaling 265,352 tons in operations ranging from Alexandria to Gibraltar."[21]

It is because of these types of successes that, by the end of the Second World War, some element of MIW whether in the form of high-speed boats, mini-submarines, or naval commandos, had been utilized by every major navy involved in the war. MIW units continued to demonstrate the ability to influence naval affairs while realizing disproportionately large results in relation to their size. Technology,

---

[21] Kemp, *Underwater Warriors*, 22.

initiative, and forward thinking had allowed men dedicated to the irregular approach the opportunity to exploit the advantages offered by maritime irregular warfare operations. In the process this enabled innovative MIW units to affect the naval balance and the course of conflict both at sea, and ashore.

Since the end of World War II, maritime irregular warfare has continued to be routinely employed around the globe. For example, elements of the unconventional approach to naval warfare have been utilized in the Korean War, the Second Indochina War (1965-1973), the Arab-Israeli Wars, and most recently in the Persian Gulf War. Maritime irregular warfare has also played an important role in many of the less publicized and smaller confrontations that have characterized the later half of the twentieth century. Examples of MIW used in this context occurred during the 1982 Falklands War, Eritrea's thirty-year fight for independence from Ethiopia, and the current terrorist-insurgent campaign being carried out in Sri Lanka by Tamil separatists. In addition to these must be added MIW's many peacetime applications. Both the United States and the Soviet Union used sophisticated MIW related tools and techniques as a means of collecting information on one another during the Cold War. North Korea's use of midget submarines and specially configured merchant marine vessels to infiltrate South Korea and Japan is a well-documented, and continuing, threat.[22] Other, less obvious uses of the indirect approach at sea include very sophisticated entrepreneurial forms of MIW best illustrated by maritime piracy and the maritime components of the drug trade. Today, the MIW concept continues to be called upon to fill a variety of traditional and nontraditional functions. In the process, both conventionally trained sailors and common criminals have exploited the advantages and opportunities that MIW and the indirect approach afford. Although much of the equipment and many of the tactics have evolved over the years, the inherent qualities that make MIW effective are as relevant today as they were fifty years ago.

B. CURRENT TRENDS IN MARITIME IRREGULAR WARFARE

In general, over the past fifty years the types of operations MIW forces have performed throughout the oceans, seas and inland waters of the world remain relatively consistent. Naval guerrillas still rely on individually

---

[22] Reference Joseph Bermudez, *DPRK Seaborne Infiltration Operations: June-December 1998*, available from http://www.nyu.edu/globalbeat/asia/bermudez010799.html, and Richard Sharpe, ed., *Jane's Fighting Ships: 1999-2000*, (Jane's Information Group Inc, 1999), 405 for information on DPRK auxiliary vessels and 401 for information on Yugo and P-4 midget submarine design characteristics capabilities.

equipped combat swimmers or unconventional submarine platforms for subsurface attacks on shipping and for infiltrating forces ashore. Small, high-speed boats in the same tradition of the World War II PT boats continue to offer surface mobility, insertion, and interdiction functions. To this day naval commandos fully dedicated to conducting maritime special operations still conduct amphibious raids, unconventional warfare, and clandestine reconnaissance operations in the littorals. In addition to being able to conduct operations on land or at sea, MIW has also incorporated some elements of aviation in order to rapidly deliver assets and/or forces. This capability has greatly extended MIW's operational reach and provided additional flexibility for the application of the indirect approach to naval warfare. Within each of the three mediums that MIW operates, sea-air-land, the most modern MIW related concepts currently being employed need to be briefly examined in order to firmly fix MIW's position in naval affairs. These current trends may provide valuable insight into the general direction MIW is heading and the kinds of capabilities MIW will be able to provide in the near-term future.

1. Mastering the Sea, Air, and Land

Today, maritime irregular warfare is as committed to the fundamental need to accelerate the shoot, move, and communicate cycle as any modern form of warfare. With the aid of technological advancements MIW has taken major evolutionary steps toward better mastery of the sea-air-land mediums, and especially in the littorals where those three mediums converge. Currently, two trends appear to be dominating maritime irregular warfare thinking.

a) *Multi-Medium Capabilities*

The ability to operate seamlessly throughout naval warfare's three different mediums has been one hallmark of the MIW operations. In the age of sail this trend was characterized by unconventional operations that combined the use of sea and land forces to achieve objectives. In modern times land and sea operations have been joined by subsurface and air operations as technological advances have allowed MIW to adapt and expand into all aspects of the naval environment. Today, MIW forces continue to try and field more efficient and effective multi-medium capabilities in order to increase the total number of options available to planners opting for an unconventional solution.

The term multi-medium capability describes the ability to utilize the three different mediums that enclose naval warfare, sea-air-land, through different combinations of assets. World War II provides an example of this trend when the Italian 10th Light Flotilla used specially configured submarines as mothercraft to launch MTB's for surface attacks on Allied shipping. Another example of this capability could take the form of using an aircraft to deliver a surface asset close to an intended target by air-dropping a small, high-speed boat and complement of personnel at sea. This surface asset could then be used to infiltrate the target area and insert a small force ashore for an offensive operation or scouting mission. This unique multi-medium capability allows MIW to be extremely flexible by being tailored to the task. Air delivery systems give MIW forces the ability to operate at extended ranges and within condensed timelines. Unconventional surface or subsurface infiltration reduces the chances of early detection. The flexibility of sending a small force ashore in an unorthodox manner thus allows MIW forces to insert when and where they are least expected.

When the individual capabilities MIW has developed overtime are appropriate for the situation and sequenced correctly the measurable impact and probability of success have proven to increase dramatically. This allows MIW to be more operationally dynamic, and capabilities to be packaged in the form of a distributed, vice focused, threat that is much harder to counter. In modern times, the number of different variations on this theme, ranging from on or below the surface of the water, air delivery capabilities, and MIW operations ashore, has allowed MIW to master the naval environment with the same ubiquitous presence that Sir Francis Drake displayed in the 16th century.

b)   *Hybrid Platforms*

Maritime irregular warfare's desire to exploit every aspect of its operating environment has in turn also given rise to a new generation of hybrid platforms. These platforms come in an infinite number of shapes and sizes and offer an equally diverse number of capabilities that make it easier for MIW forces to mount effective unconventional operations. This thesis will divide the different types of hybrid platforms into three general categories.

First, perhaps the most sophisticated of the hybrid platforms are those that can transition between mediums during operations. One example of this type of hybrid platform is the North Korean high-speed infiltration craft (HSIC/PBF).[23] At a length of 12.8m and a top surface speed of roughly 45kt, the HSIC is similar in appearance to a small surface craft. "Large numbers [*were*] built for Agent infiltration and covert operations. These craft have a very low radar cross-section and 'squat' at high speeds...[*In addition, the HSIC*] is alleged to be able to submerge to a depth of 3m using a snort mast, and to propel dived at 4kt."[24]

Although crude in comparison to similar platforms developed by wealthier nations, the HSIC does provide an excellent example of the drift within MIW towards hybrid platforms capable of transitioning from one form of operation to another. Illustrated in this example by the HSIC's ability to transition directly and uninterrupted from surface operations to subsurface operations. The HSIC example also proves that these innovations do not reside solely in the domain of the premier navies. In order to avoid detection South American drug cartels looking for new ways to smuggle their product into the United States have

---

[23] Sharpe, *Jane's Fighting Ships: 1999-2000,* 412.

[24] *Ibid.,* 412

also utilized a vessel with similar design features,[25] in addition to experimenting with sophisticated mini-submarines.[26] Additionally, if MIW is to maintain mastery of the littorals it will require improved coastal and hinterland mobility. This need could spawn a family of light vehicles capable of directly transitioning from sea to land operations and offers another example of the trend towards fielding more capable hybrid platforms.

Another variation of the hybrid concept that has already been alluded to but needs further explanation involves configuring larger conventional platforms to support and launch smaller MIW assets. Since World War II, conventional submarines have had the ability to launch and recover smaller mini-submarines while remaining submerged. Additionally, surface vessels with conventional design characteristics continue to adapt to the primary role of delivering smaller unconventional assets. These types of operations allow MIW forces to operate at extended ranges, for longer durations and represent another distinct family

---

[25] Reference Jane's Defense Weekly available at http://jdw.janes.com for information on low profile maritime drug smuggling platforms called, "Super Smugglers."

[26] New York Times Company, *210 Miles From Pacific Ocean, Drug Smugglers Try to Build Sub*, The New York Times, 8 September 2000, late edition (east coast).

of hybrid platforms currently in inventory and designed specifically for conducting MIW operations.

One final variation of the hybrid concept needs to be briefly identified. Not all practitioners of MIW can field state-of-the-art equipment and capabilities. This fact has led some groups to pursue alternative paths to increased capabilities through the development of hybrid platforms produced by combining existing technologies. During Eritrea's thirty-year fight for independence from Ethiopia, the Eritirean People's Liberation Front (EPLF) successfully deployed this type of hybrid platform and a very effective MIW strategy against the Ethiopian Navy.[27] The EPLF's high-speed gunboat was fashioned by mounting a twin 20mm anti-aircraft weapon on a 20ft fiberglass hull powered by dual outboard engines. These boats were then used along the coast for interdiction operations and to support small raids ashore. Unable to purchase MIW specific systems the EPLF combined readily available and low-cost civilian boat hulls with crew served weapons captured in the field from the Ethiopian Army. Although the types of weapons mounted in

---

[27] For information on Eritrea's thirty-year fight for independence see Dan Connell, *Against All Odds: A Chronicle of the Eritrean Revolution* (Red Sea Press, 1993), and Christopher Clapham, ed., *African Guerrillas* (Indiana University Press, 1998).

each boat varied the EPLF was able to develop a rugged, reliable, and very capable unconventional platform by combining existing off-the-shelf components with other weapon systems on hand. Individually none of the systems that went into building this platform could be classified as state-of-the-art. It was the end product and the way in which it was employed that made the EPLF's hybrid gunboat cutting edge. During the Iran-Iraq War, the Iranians deployed a very similar unconventional high-speed capability.[28]

C.   LINKING THE REGULAR AND IRREGULAR APPROACH

In order to gain a complete understanding of the MIW concept and tie together the various forms it has taken over time, the overarching themes that guide MIW must be clearly identified. In the previous sections the advantages of MIW were discussed and many elements inherent to MIW operations were highlighted. Each of these points plays an important role in the overall understanding of the maritime irregular warfare concept. Although the points brought out in the typology form the foundation on which MIW stands, the sheer

---

[28] Reference Jane's Intelligence Review, *The Tanker War*, Jane's Information Group Limited, 1 May 1992, for information about Iranian Boghammer operations during the Iran-Iraq War and Sharpe, *Jane's Fighting Ships: 1999-2000*, 329 for design characteristics and capabilities.

diversity found in the irregular approach to naval warfare precludes the use of these elements as a way of tying the MIW concept together. Instead, two broader, overarching themes must be derived from the typology that take into account these points while continuing to simplify MIW conceptually.

Figure 2 is a graphical representation of the approach this thesis has taken to arrive at an explanation of the MIW concept. Due to MIW's diversity and range, a precisely worded definition or list of principles that collectively define the MIW concept is impossible to produce. MIW is a concept that must be gradually distilled from numerous sources. This process begins at the lower level of the MIW pyramid formed by the MIW typology.

The advantages of MIW and the various elements of MIW brought out in that discussion form the foundation for understanding the MIW concept. This step-by-step process continues by bringing MIW up to date and examining its current global posture and direction. The corollary hypothesis discussed below will further refine MIW conceptually. When these three levels of the MIW pyramid are taken together and combined, a clearer understanding of the MIW concept begins to emerge.

```
                         MIW
                       Concept

                   MIW and Sea Power
                  (Corollary Hypothesis)

                 Current Trends in MIW

                     MIW Typology
                     (Key Traits)
```

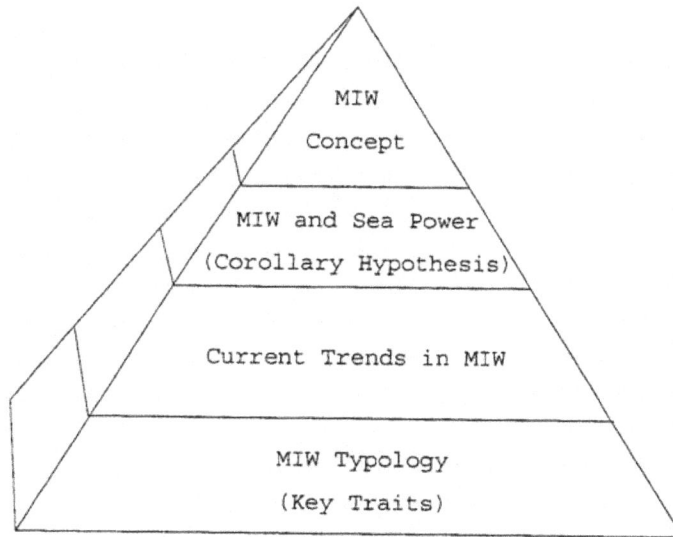

Figure 2. The Maritime Irregular Warfare Pyramid

The tight linkage and interplay between MIW and
conventional naval warfare is a critical part of the MIW
concept. This interdependent relationship is actually
comprised of two key parts. The first is that, when the
typology is taken as a whole, it becomes obvious that right
alongside the evolution in conventional naval warfare, comes
progress and advancement in the unconventional sphere. This
point is most easily understood by realizing that the
continuous advancements in conventional naval warfare have
been aimed at gaining an increased capability or naval
advantage. This increased capability has the effect of

36

forcing opponents, or competitors, to meet these new challenges by exploring new, unorthodox avenues of attack and accelerating the rise of the irregular approach. At the same time, these advances in technology and capability have increasingly led to the need for specially trained personnel and equipment to fulfill the MIW requirement. This relationship suggests that advance in the conventional sphere leads directly to opportunity and advancement in the unconventional sphere as new weapons become vulnerable, and new operational methods enable the employment of the indirect approach.

The second part of this interdependent relationship between the regular and irregular forms of naval warfare concerns the bond linking MIW directly to sea power. MIW has consistently been employed, either independently or as an integrated part of regular naval warfare strategies, as a means of projecting sea power and gaining sea control. Depending on the location and particular situation, sea control can be a prerequisite for larger strategies involving land-based objectives. When thinking about the advantages of MIW this is the area that readily comes to mind, and historically this is the arena in which MIW has proven its worth. The offensive nature of naval warfare and the need for decisive operations to gain sea control for the most part determine the character of MIW operations.[29] The role of the Italian 10th Light Flotilla during World War II is an outstanding example of a sophisticated MIW organization designed specifically around the idea of gaining control of the sea, or alternatively, for negating the Allies absolute control of the sea through unconventional sea denial operations. Offensively oriented, Decima Mas offered Italy a low-cost and effective alternative for challenging the Allies conventional superiority in the Mediterranean.[30] One point of contention brought out in the typology is that MIW can affect conflict both at sea and ashore. When properly employed, MIW has proven to possess this dual potential. The point being made here is that the primary linkages that support MIW and tie it into a cohesive military strategy extends directly to sea power and control of the sea.

---

[29] Wayne Hughes, *Fleet Tactics and Coastal Combat* (Naval Institute Press, 2000).

[30] Although MIW operations are primarily offensive in nature as this passage points out, the Liberation Tigers of Tamil Eelam (LTTE) are currently using a strategically defensive MIW strategy spearheaded by small, fast gunboats and an amphibious raiding capability to maintained control over the Jaffna Peninsula and counter the Sri Lankan Navy (SLN) in the north. While tactically offensive, it is important to point out that MIW can be used defensively at the strategic level. Reference: Rohan Gunaratna, *Sri Lanka's Ethnic Crisis and National Security* (Colombo: South Asian Network on Conflict Research, 1998).

Additionally, this relationship suggests that MIW operations be tightly connected to the water and the exploitation of the water flank as a means of gaining advantage and achieving objectives. This goes far beyond the use of water simply as an avenue of approach or convenient escape route. In this heightened sense, water becomes MIW's primary enabler and operational center of gravity. These fundamental points shape the interdependent relationship between the regular and irregular approach, and together comprise an overarching theme that is consistently found in maritime irregular warfare operations.

THIS PAGE INTENTIONALLY LEFT BLANK

III. INFORMATION AGE CONFLICT

There is no single answer to the many challenges
that will present themselves in the future, *naval
forces*[31] will have to adapt as they have done
throughout history to changing circumstances...At
the same time, the fact that the future is
uncertain is no excuse for failing to make
adequate preparations.

          - Operational Maneuver From The Sea

A.   THE NATURE OF THE BEAST

In order to develop a viable vision of MIW's future,
the coming trends in information age conflict must be
identified in a clear and simplified manner that adds value,
and remains relevant, to the overall discussion. This
chapter approaches the future of warfare's inherent
complexities by combining the insights and analysis of
existing research in an analytical framework for presenting
crisis, conflict, and war in the information age. In
developing this general vision the most widely accepted
categories for interpreting the future of warfare will be
used in order to build an accurate and realistic framework.
This chapter will then derive an alternative, evolutionary
based interpretation that may offer a more powerful

---

[31] Emphasis added.

perspective of information age conflict in the early decades of the twenty-first century.

B.   BACKGROUND AND BASIC APPROACH

A vast literature dedicated to thinking about the future of warfare already exists.[32] Because of the depth of this existing literature, this chapter essentially provides a condensed stocktaking of the most relevant concepts and themes consistently found throughout this rich body of work. As previously stated the primary goal of this chapter is to synthesize the core concepts found in the existing literature into a clearly defined, and useable, framework for interpreting information age conflict. The points with MIW relevance developed using this framework will then serve to inform the concluding chapter of this thesis.

The "conflict in the information age" framework will be limited to identifying broader, overarching issues, and will be presented in essentially an outline format comprised of

---

[32] e.g. Bevin Alexander, *The Future of Warfare* (New York NY: W.W. Norton and Company, 1995), John Arquilla and David Ronfeldt, eds., *In Athena's Camp* (Santa Monica CA: RAND, 1997), George and Meredith Friedman, *The Future of War* (New York NY: Crown Publishers, 1996), Robert Pfaltzgraff and Richard Shultz, eds., *War in the Information Age* (Duller VA: Brassey's Books, 1997), Robert Scales, *Future Warfare* (Carlisle Barracks PA: U.S. Army War College, 1999), and Martin Van Creveld, *The Transformation of War* (New York NY: The Free Press, 1991), etc.

three primary components: 1) the emerging geostrategic setting; 2) the revolution in military affairs (RMA); and finally, tactical technology trends (T3). Figure 3 offers a graphic representation of the framework's three primary components, and the interdependent relationships currently being forged by advances in information technology.

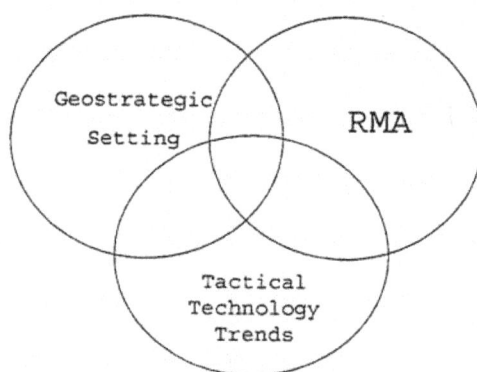

Figure 3. Conflict in the Information Age Framework

Approaching the subject in this manner offers two distinct advantages. First, the themes developed in this chapter have purposefully been chosen because of their timeless and dynamic qualities that avoid built-in obsolescence or the construction of a brittle and narrowly focused framework. Ultimately, in order for any framework to be effective it must be able to handle tough tests by being flexible enough to adjust for extreme cases, and/or potential wild card scenarios. And second, concentrating on the broader overarching themes and their linkages eliminates the need for a static, laundry list of topics with limited applicability and no long-term strategic value.

Prior to beginning this analysis some important issues and assumptions need to be isolated in order to shape the context, and define the limits, of the following discussion:

1. This thesis begins by recognizing that, "In the absence of a relatively fixed, strategic environment, we are faced with a far more complex world that defies authoritative forecasts of the future."[33]

2. There is no single answer to crises, conflict and war in the future. This point and the preceding point are complementary, and the volume of material that attempts to make sense of the future of warfare supports this notion. Instead this thesis acknowledges that, "we are in a period of great transition. The changes experienced in the few years following the end of the Cold War will likely continue. In their wake will follow crises, conflict, and war."[34]

3. This thesis focuses on, but is not limited to, the near-term future. The reason for choosing this benchmark is so that the intellectual beacon can be placed far enough in front of the pace of change to avoid being constricted by the current environment.

4. The framework developed in this chapter acts only as an outline for simplifying and organizing critical environmental variables. The strength of the framework is

---

[33] Training and Doctrine Command (*TRADOC*), *Pam 525-5*, available from http://www-tradoc.army.mil/tpubs/pams/p525-5.htm, Aug 1994, 1.

[34] *Ibid.*, 2.

its ability to break the subject down into its component parts for closer scrutiny, and its ability to remain flexible and adjust for rapid changes and environmental uncertainty.

C.   THE EMERGING GEOSTRATEGIC SETTING

Crisis, conflict, and war do not take place in a vacuum, but within a constantly evolving geopolitical framework that provides focus and intensity. In order to understand the trends in information age conflict we must first try to make sense of the broader arena in which these actions take place. This dictates that forecasting the emerging geostrategic setting form the first step in any investigation into the future of warfare.

With the dissolution of the Soviet Union the relatively fixed bi-polar strategic environment that characterized the Cold War has given way to a multi-polar, regionally focused, international security system that is far more complex.[35] Concurrently, the acceleration and

---

[35] This thesis recognizes that while the U.S. is currently the only superpower in the world, history teaches this enviable position is unlikely to be permanent. While the U.S. will retain its mantle of leadership into the near future, that leadership position will become increasingly complex and more difficult to maintain due to the probable rise of one or more major regional competitors. Although the exact form these competitors will take remains unclear, and no mirror image peer competitor to the U.S. is expected to emerge, major competitors will acquire the ability to challenge U.S. interests regionally, and to a selective degree, globally. This thesis argues that "multi-polar" is

diffusion of advanced technologies and weapons continue to fundamentally alter and reshape the world around us. Together these two critical events have combined to produce a geostrategic setting in flux as it transitions from the industrial age of the twentieth century into the information age of the twenty-first century.

Clouded by this environmental uncertainty, the future of warfare remains difficult to project. Nevertheless, countless futurists have tried to predict the general parameters of the twenty-first century.

> One is a vision of the future devoid of major war – a century of peace. This school argues that due to an expanded number of democratic states, shared understanding – through advances in information technology, and global economic interdependence, we are entering a new era where War is no longer deemed a productive means of pursuing strategic objectives. Even if history proves this prediction correct, it will also show that the transition from the world's bloodiest century to one of relative peace was not smooth.[36]

In fact this rosy vision of the future may ignore a fundamental truth consistently found in the past. As the world's geopolitical framework continues to undergo fundamental restructuring accompanied by dramatic alterations across the technical, societal, economic,

---

the most accurate description of the emerging geostrategic setting.

[36] *Ibid.*, 5.

religious, cultural, and physical spectrum, history teaches that change of this magnitude and intensity serves to increase global tension and instability. Far from reaching the "century of peace," the geostrategic cycle can be thought of as having merely reached the uncertain, and momentary, plateau that usually precedes any major shift in the strategic landscape. At the very least, it should be noted that, "the types of crises and conflicts we have experienced since the end of the Cold War will likely continue into the early decades of the twenty-first century."[37] A brief discussion of the two primary forces at work in the operating environment is offered in order to further break out and clarify the emerging geostrategic setting.

1. The Geostrategic Reordering

Current sources of conflict - ethnic rivalries, nationalism, religion-based antagonisms, and competition for scarce economic resources, including water - will continue and perhaps intensify. Transnational threats such as international crime syndicates, terrorist networks, and drug cartels also have the potential to grow in strength and influence, presenting security problems that are significantly different from those of the past in terms of scope and quality. A higher incidence of failed states, coupled with the aforementioned sources of conflict and unpredictable natural and human-induced disasters, will likely lead to a rise in

---

[37] *Ibid.*, 1.

regional instability. Maintaining international stability will probably require a higher frequency of action by the international community.[38]

A large proportion of the outside literature dedicated to interpreting the future of warfare, and all of the current projects supported by the Department of Defense (DOD), paint a picture of the emerging geostrategic setting similar to the one presented here.[39] Accepting this basic outline, this excerpt provides the necessary information, and sufficient depth of analysis, to identify the major fault lines emerging in the geostrategic setting. In particular, the simultaneous increase in the number of internal breakdowns and the rise of aggressive non-state threats,[40] two trends that ultimately feed off of one another, appear to be driving the geostrategic reordering.

To begin with, although this compressed view of the future does possess elements of significant change, it is important to highlight the fact that it also suggests many fundamental aspects will remain essentially unchanged during

---

[38] *Army After Next (AAN) Annual Report FY98*, 1998, 1.

[39] e.g. The Army After Next (AAN), . . .From The Sea, Operational Maneuver From The Sea, Global Reach, Global Power, Army Vision 2010.

[40] Although the term "transnational" threat is referenced this thesis applies a broader term, non-state threat, in order to encompass transnational, subnational, and anational threats.

the timeframe in question. This translates into continued activity throughout the low-intensity spectrum and in other forms of conflict below the conventional threshold. All told, the current sources of crisis, conflict, and war and their many variations do not appear to be receding through the thirty-year mark.

Added to this already volatile mixture is the rise of non-state threats. Several authors have even taken this general vision of the future a step further by suggesting that it represents the beginning of a new, "bifurcated"[41] international system no longer dominated by the state-centered paradigm. This new bifurcated system they identify is comprised primarily of the traditional state-centered paradigm, while recognizing the presence of a potentially destabilizing non-state stratum made up of international crime organizations, ethnic/religious separatists, and transnational terrorist organizations. This school of thought points out the fact that, "the Clausewitzian *trinitarian* concept of warfare – centering on the state, the government, and the population – has been supplemented, though not replaced, by a system in which the state is

---

[41] Pfaltzgraff & Shultz, eds., *War in the Information Age: New Challenges for U.S. Security*, 11.

either weakened or has disintegrated."[42] To support their claim these authors cite the breakup of numerous states into smaller newer states, increasing frequency of failed states, and instances in which states only maintain nominal control over their population, and territory.

Clearly these new, well-organized, better-informed, and lethally armed non-state entities increase the complexity of the geostrategic landscape. This new dynamic also lends credence and fits nicely with the argument that in the future asymmetrical/asynchronous forces similar in appearance to these non-state threats and utilizing indirect methods of operation could pose a serious problem to a more conventionally focused adversary. When combined with the threat posed by the intensification of "ism's,"[43] along with other natural and human-induced sources of conflict, these characteristics also have the potential to alter and reorder the way the geostrategic landscape has traditionally been viewed.[44]

---

[42] *Ibid.*, 10.

[43] i.e. Non-state threats combined with ethno-nationalism, terrorism, and/or religious fundamentalism.

[44] Robert Kaplan, *The Coming Anarchy*, The Atlantic Monthly, February, 1994.

2.   The Rapid Pace of Technological Change

Superimposed on this changing geostrategic framework is the rapid pace of technological change. Countless conflicting theories have been put forward about the impact information technologies will have on the future of warfare. Collectively, the only thing these theories convey is the sentiment that, "Despite common acknowledgement of the fundamental changes in the strategic environment, little agreement exists about how information technologies will further affect it."[45]

Technologically speaking, "diffusion" and "connectedness" are the two watchwords for the coming years. Interestingly, these two terms can also be related back to the two primary trends identified in the geostrategic reordering. The disintegration of the state, or the state no longer being needed, represents a form of diffusion while connectedness can be found in the ways non-state actors are increasingly able to reach across traditional boundaries. In other words, diffusion and connectedness are likely to change the way peoples group and not just how they communicate. This has major implications for the future

---

[45] Pfaltzgraff, & Shultz, eds., *War in the Information Age: New Challenges for U.S. Security*, 332.

scope of war. Thought of in these terms, both actually define a single global phenomenon embracing the strategic environment. That phenomenon involves the spread of sophisticated information technologies along with the advanced information architecture linking these systems together. The momentum behind this phenomenon itself poses challenges, since both "diffusion" and "connectedness," along with the process they help define, act as enablers for various forms of information warfare (IW). Here again the outside literature provides the best description of IW and its potential impact on the future.

> The increasing proliferation of information technology provides potential adversaries – whether nations, organizations, or individuals – with the capability to conduct increasingly sophisticated information operations. . .Potential adversaries do not need high-technology or strictly military systems to conduct information warfare. The ability to manipulate, isolate, or negate portions of the electromagnetic spectrum will be a key element of future military operations. Disruption of the opponent's ability to use these systems while protecting [ones] own will prove crucial in the future.[46]

There has been a lot of speculation regarding the rise in information warfare because, by design, the infosphere has proven to be porous and prone to attack. In the high technology arena oftentimes the most cutting edge

---

[46] Training and Doctrine Command (TRADOC), Pam 525-5, Aug 1994, ch. 2,p. 6.

technologies can become the most vulnerable and the easiest to counteract. Current events support this argument, and point to the emergence of new types of military strategies aimed at disruption and paralysis instead of the more traditional strategies of attrition and annihilation. In this heightened sense, winning by paralysis may begin to take on new meaning and importance in future military affairs.

Because IW's full strength has not yet been put to the test, like many of the new concepts being generated by the information age, it is still an amorphous concept with no clearly agreed upon definition. As an example, the IW label has been applied to everything from non-lethal attacks on the civilian infrastructure, to strategic psychological operations, to more conventional military-against-military confrontations in which precision guidance and improved strike capabilities elevate warfare to a new level by dramatically increasing combat power.

No cursory analysis can do a field as complicated and technical as IW justice, many books and countless articles have been dedicated to the subject, and still its enigmatic character persists. Without question, the field of IW will continue to experience quantum leaps in capability through the near-term future. While recognizing IW's importance and latent potential this thesis limits the discussion to making a macro-level distinction between the "independent" versus "integrated" forms of information warfare. Limiting the discussion to this level of analysis avoids identifying IW capabilities that will be rapidly surpassed and instead casts IW in the role of another tool emerging in crisis, conflict, and war.

> Independent IW can be an alternative to war, as, for example, when civilian targets and information systems are attacked by terrorists; or it can be used in preemptive strikes on systems supporting military operations. At the same time, integrated IW can be viewed as part of the transformation of battlefield military operations, in which information technologies are used to support traditional military objectives by providing enhanced situational awareness for conducting operations, with all the attendant changes in organization and doctrine that this will require. These two kinds of IW can be conducted simultaneously or separately, depending on who is engaged in a conflict.[47]

Clearly, the overall effect of technological change on crisis, conflict, and war will be hard to gauge. Only time will be able to bring the subject into better focus. Be that as it may, there seems to be an overwhelming consensus among observers that the fundamental reordering described above, along with other rapid advances in technology, will coalesce to form the backbone of the emerging geostrategic setting.

---

[47] Pfaltzgraff, & Shultz, eds., *War in the Information Age: New Challenges for U.S. Security*, 333.

Additionally, this thesis argues that the future geostrategic environment will become increasingly complex, characterized by shifting balances within regions and the prevalence of ad-hoc security structures, ultimately leading to greater instability, and increasing the likelihood of crisis, conflict, and war especially in areas below the conventional threshold of war.

D.   THE REVOLUTION IN MILITARY AFFAIRS

In conjunction with the changes taking place in the geostrategic setting, it appears that the foundation for an information-based RMA is being built simultaneously. The vast quantity of recent literature dedicated to investigating the future of warfare has greatly expanded and clouded what is meant by the term RMA. It should once again be pointed out that, like IW, there is currently no clearly defined or widely accepted definition, and that this thesis does not seek to become mired down trying to create one. Instead the main effort will continue to focus on identifying the overarching trends that are consistently cited as products of the emerging RMA.

Prior to identifying these trends some additional amplifying information is addressed in order to hone this chapter's use of the term RMA, and how it has been portrayed in the scholarly literature to date. Additionally, a two-tiered approach is offered as a way to frame the subject for discussion, and act as a primer for interpreting the trends in military affairs.

1.   The RMA as a Concept

One feature of the RMA is that it is currently being misused to describe many common evolutionary changes that are not revolutionary in nature. In order to put the RMA in its proper context it is important to be able to distinguish between the evolutionary and revolutionary changes in military affairs. This thesis relies on a very general distinction between the two:

> Evolution is the logical progression of an existing system or framework, while revolution connotes a fundamental break with precedent...a truly revolutionary strategic development alters perceptions of the relationship of means to ends and, most importantly, dictates a reformulation of warfighting doctrine...[48]

This thesis sides with the scholarly literature that believes many of the advances currently being credited as proof of an RMA are in actuality merely evolutionary steps brought about by technological advances. Although the effect of these advances in technology may have an impact on military affairs, by themselves they will not lead to a RMA

---

[48] Arquilla, & Ronfeldt, eds., *In Athena's Camp: Preparing for Conflict in the Information Age*, 80.

until coupled with other long-term operational and organizational issues. Several of these purely technology-based prime movers will be addressed in the tactical technology trends section later in the chapter.

Almost all the participants in the RMA debate currently recognize that this is but the latest in a historical series of RMAs, and that no two RMAs are exactly alike. One thing past RMAs offer is an abundant amount of data and information upon which to reflect. With the aid of the historical record, and in spite of the RMA's soft definition, there seems to be a consensus that in general RMA's include four primary elements. These four constituent elements include, "new military technologies or systems and involve complex operational and organizational issues; but few agree on the priority among these four elements and identity of *the* key driver (if only one exists)."[49] Additionally, the RMA's current status continues to be called into question for, "while the community largely agrees that there is an RMA to be pursued, whether it is already in progress, is about to start, or is mature and about to end all have adherents."[50]

---

[49] *Ibid.*, 99.

[50] *Ibid.*, 100.

This thesis maintains that with the aid of advanced information technologies the RMA is currently in its initial stages of development and that the final outcome lies somewhere in the future. Concurrently, this chapter will suggest that while a RMA may be attainable within the next thirty years, a two-tiered approach is needed in order to organize the RMA's four elements and make sense of the rapid changes taking place in military affairs.

2. A Two-tiered Approach to the RMA

The two-tiered approach begins by accepting at face value the four constituent traits commonly found in past RMA's and then proceeds to separate those traits with a greater near-term effect from those with a greater long-term effect. Doing so emphasizes the fact that a RMA is not a single discrete event but a process that develops over time.

a) The Near-Term Phase

The near-term phase of the present RMA centers on its first two variables, technologies and evolving military systems. These are the types of military advances that are the closest at hand and the easiest to grasp conceptually. They are characterized, "by the technologies demonstrated during the Gulf War: stealth, precision weapons, advanced sensors, C4I, and the use of real-time (or near-real-time) space systems."[51] Some proponents argue that, together, advances in these two fields are capable of producing an outright RMA. And in their defense, purely technology-driven RMA's, although rare, have been cited in the past. The fundamental changes in warfare that followed the introduction of the longbow and gunpowder are the two commonly cited examples of such RMA's. Presently this is the area that has dominated most people's understanding of the RMA and led to the perception that RMA's are primarily technology-driven events. It should be pointed out that a majority of the literature reviewed does not share this myopic interpretation. Although technologies and evolving military systems will bring new forces to bear within military affairs, most doubt that by themselves they will achieve a fundamental break with tradition or the "order of magnitude or more" increase in military effectiveness most point to as a litmus test for measuring RMA's. Other detractors of this view also point out the fact that merely inserting advanced technologies into existing systems and organizational structures, which is currently what occurs, ignores the crucial third and fourth RMA variables and can actually introduce inefficiencies into military operations

---

[51] *Ibid.*, 124.

creating additional uncertainty. Referring to this situation most involved in the RMA debate tend to advance the argument that, "technology alone is not sufficient to produce a military revolution; how military organizations adapt and shape new technology, military systems, and operational concepts is much more important."[52]

b) *The Long-Term Phase*

The long-term phase is encapsulated in the idea that "concepts are stronger than tools," and therefore focuses on the last two variables commonly attributed to the RMA: namely, operational innovation and organizational adaptation. It would appear from the literature that this is the area that holds the key to any future RMA, meanwhile there is still considerable debate about when, and if, this phase can even be reached. While there has been tangible evidence of progress in the near-term phase of the RMA, real progress in the long-term arena has yet to materialize outside of isolated, and rigidly controlled, experimentation.[53] Many involved in the RMA debate still contend that until the technologically based near-term

---

[52] *Ibid.*, 81.

[53] e.g. Advanced warfighting experiments like Sea Dragon, Quantum Leap, Force XXI.

advances are translated into operational and organizational terms, the RMA will remain incomplete.

This project does not have the space necessary to engage in the organizational jiu-jitsu, or cover the endless number of wire diagram permutations, needed to explain the shift away from hierarchical structures towards flatter, non-hierarchical structures that can result in increased information flows. Nor is it necessary for this thesis' purposes to list all the different forms operational innovation could take. That level of analysis is not necessary for identifying the trends in military affairs this thesis is focused on. Suffice it to say the exact nature of these long-term advances in the operational and organizational sphere remains hazy and inchoate at best. However, together with the near-term variables and the arguments presented in the geostrategic setting section, some distinct trends in military affairs are emerging that help tie together the RMA's four variables and summarize the RMA debate for the timeframe in question.

3.   The Trends in Military Affairs

From the contemporary RMA debate it appears that several identifiable trends are emerging in military affairs. The points made here serve only to illuminate the general direction crisis, conflict, and war is taking in the information age, not to indicate an absolute direction. These trends are classified into two separate categories and are again defined using broad strokes.

a) The High-technology Trends

One hallmark of past RMA's has been the continuing expansion of the arena in which conflict takes place, commonly referred to now as the battlespace. As military platforms, the submarine and the airplane both added two new dimensions to warfare and are classic examples of this historical phenomenon. Today, elements of an expanding battlespace are being identified as well. For example,

> in the emerging RMA, long-range precision strike and the information aspects of war will fundamentally transform war on land, sea, and in the air, while adding two new warfare areas: space warfare and information warfare, both independent and integrated. The common theme will be the overlapping of battlespace and multidimensionality, creating integrated air, land, sea, space, and information operations.[54]

Although we cannot definitively predict the exact direction a future conflict might take, we can certainly expect to witness a significant broadening of the battlespace in these two general areas. As with previous expansion in the battlespace, this one will also lead to the

---

[54] Pfaltzgraff, & Shultz, eds., *War in the Information Age: New Challenges for U.S. Security*, 344.

creation of additional avenues of attack. MIW's continuing desire to field more efficient and effective multi-medium capabilities is an extension of this same basic concept.

Another subject of the current RMA centers on the idea of battlespace transparency. Advocates of its potential posit that, "the emerging RMA will create a transparent battlefield in which commanders, and even troops in field units, will be able to see the whole battlespace in real time."[55] The creation of greater battlespace transparency has also been referred to as improved situational awareness. And it should be stressed that although this may serve as a useful goal to strive for, achieving total and continuous situational awareness in war is highly unlikely. As numerous authors like to point out, the principles of chance, friction, and the "fog of war," all complex human driven phenomena, will not be negated by a simple engineering solution. Additionally, "low-technology adversaries likely to be encountered in OOTW[56] may be able to develop indirect methods of aggression that circumvent [these] capabilities."[57] Here again it can be said that along with

---

[55] *Ibid.*, 344-345.

[56] Operations Other Than War (OOTW).

[57] *Ibid.*, 345.

many advantages, advanced technology always comes with exploitable disadvantages that observant opponents are quick to grasp. Regardless of the degree of situational awareness technology can produce, it can be assumed that warfare will continue to be a dynamic process that is situationally and opponent dependent.

Many commentators have combined the preceding two points to argue that technology is ushering in a new era of increased operational tempo. Those involved in this debate maintain that the acceleration of time, more aptly the ability to operate inside an opponent's decision cycle,[58] may become the deciding factor in the future by compressing the levels of war – the strategic, operational, and tactical – and delivering one of the most vital principles of war, the element of surprise. Optimally, as the observe phase of the decision cycle is radically shortened with the aid of advanced sensor technology, it becomes much easier to anticipate and react to an adversary's movements. As one author suggests,

> ...surprise may become *the* decisive factor in determining both the "course and outcome" of a

---

[58] This refers to Colonel John Boyd's well-known model of the command and control process the orient, observe, decide, and act (OODA) loop to discuss how effective command and control allows decisions to be made and acted on more rapidly than the enemy.

war; in fact, these may now be described as "a single phenomenon." As a result, the initial period may now be in effect the *only* period in future warfare. Operational campaigning under these circumstances must be viewed as an integrated, seamless process in which the time constraints of the individual elements are critical to the effectiveness of the overall plan.[59]

b) *The Highly-sophisticated Trends*

Along with the more readily identifiable trends being driven by advanced technology two other subtle trends are emerging that are less dependent on hardware. These two trends deal with the changing nature of command and the prospect of the low-tech/highly-sophisticated opponent. Although these trends are usually found in between the folds of the high technology trends, they may actually provide additional insight into the nature of crisis, conflict, and war in the future.

In order to take full advantage of the emerging technological trends the nature of command may have to fundamentally change as well. This is perhaps the least controversial area within the RMA debate, and a portion of this topic has already been covered in the long-term phase discussion. To briefly revisit the concept, many observers foresee military hierarchies becoming flatter, and more

---

[59] Arquilla, & Ronfeldt, eds., *In Athena's Camp: Preparing for Conflict in the Information Age*, 88.

streamlined, as information is quickly passed to lower echelons of command. In addition, analysts predict that in the future commanders will rely less on set movements to maintain control and instead devolve greater freedom of action to subordinate units so they can react quickly to rapidly changing situations while still fulfilling the commander's goals. The key point to take away from this discussion is the move towards decentralized tactical command, with greater strategic oversight. Concurrently, in the best case scenario technology and the changing nature of command will combine to increase the lethality of the small unit by allowing for a better exploitation of the tactical situation through improved information flows and fewer layers of command and control.

The second trend is better categorized as a constantly evolving phenomenon that poses the greatest threat to forces relying on high-technology advances for conventional superiority. This is the rise of an opponent using low-technology tools but a highly sophisticated, asymmetrical/asynchronous strategy to circumvent, blind, or nullify a high-tech adversary's advantage. Most participants in the RMA debate are quick to caveat many technology driven trends with examples of the problems these types of opponents will present. For example observers point out that by monitoring high-tech developments, low-tech competitors will probably be able to develop creative asymmetric/asynchronous strategies and employ niche capabilities aimed at avoiding high-tech strengths and capitalizing on high-tech's vulnerabilities. To complicate matters further, adversaries may pursue a combination of asymmetries, or similarly several low-tech adversaries may combine to create a distributed asymmetric threat.

As more of the trends identified in the high-tech category begin to filter down through, and out of, the more advanced societies the greatest threat may not come from a similarly equipped foe, but from an asymmetric force aware of the latest technologies capabilities and limitations. Or more problematic still is a similarly equipped foe, clever and flexible enough *not* to use that equipment, instead choosing to act like a low-tech opponent. In this scenario, these low-tech/highly-sophisticated adversaries might not provide the usual signatures for these systems to track or fit the profile commonly associated with a threat. By utilizing odd and irregular strategies, and means, these types of adversaries may be able to identify pressure points and negate certain high-tech advantages.

E.   TACTICAL TECHNOLOGY TRENDS

Of the crisis, conflict, and war framework's three primary components, the RMA remains the most difficult to make sense of, or project into the future. This chapter has sought to clarify the main body of the RMA debate by better defining the use of the term and identifying the presence of two distinct lobes: One concentrating on near-term technology-driven trends, and the other centered on the more complex long-term operational and organizational issues that remain further in the future. By fusing the basic trends found in these two areas, this section has sought to develop a clearer picture of the general direction military affairs appears to be headed in the near-term.

Whether a full RMA can be achieved within the next thirty years is debatable. While it appears there has been real progress in many of the near-term areas, progress in the more critical long-term areas remains hard to identify or even define. Even if an information age RMA is achieved in the near-term, not everyone will be able to take full advantage of it. While pursuit of the RMA may be out of reach for some, the comparatively low investment trends addressed here may attract interest and provide an alternate means of achieving strategic objectives.

Although many aspects of the future remain indistinct, others have become discernible. This section attempts to focus greater attention on the trends emerging thanks to enhanced warfighting tools and tactics. In the absence of the RMA's long-term variables, these trends combined with those already identified in the near-term RMA phase, and those in the geostrategic setting, may offer a hedged view of crisis, conflict, and war in the information age.

One particularly strong trend has been the global push towards establishing the primacy of precision. The shift towards greater precision, and the resulting trends that are a consequence of that shift, lie at the very heart of the tactical technology trends (T3) discussion. Although commonly associated with advanced missile technology, precision-guided munitions (PGM's) can come in many different forms and offer a wide range of capabilities. No one doubts that in the future precision guidance will continue to filter from the platform level all the way down to even the most basic levels of combat. A brief excerpt describing precision's advantages on the battlefield helps emphasize this trend,

> Precision...permits the use of weapons that hit
> and kill only legitimate military targets,
> reducing collateral damage. It facilitates rapid,
> effective, and economical maneuver on the

battlefield. Precision also simplifies logistics, enhancing its usefulness to warfighters.[60]

The effectiveness of PGM's has already been demonstrated in multiple confrontations around the globe. Currently, no portion of the warfare spectrum has been left untouched by the advantages precision guidance offers. As increasing numbers of PGM's are made available many observers have postulated that their effects, either singularly or en masse, will enable the move towards the strategic *coup de main* operations mentioned at the end of the high-technology trends section.

Another area of improved tactical performance, closely related to PGM's, comes from the ability to strike targets at greater range. Many authors have offered examples of how the long-range PGM dynamic will fit into future conflicts and the changes that will follow in its wake.

> Future military forces will be increasingly able to attack concentrations of land or naval forces at long ranges. In such a lethal environment, close-combat maneuver operations will take on new forms. Units will need to be smaller and more information-intensive. Most importantly, we will think of the battlefield less in spatial terms, and more in temporal ones.[61]

---

[60] Pfaltzgraff, & Shultz, eds., *War in the Information Age: New Challenges for U.S. Security*, 349.

[61] *Ibid.*, 350.

Of particular interest is the way the T3's complement and complete many of the thoughts already brought out in the previous discussions about the geostrategic setting and RMA. The consequences of extremely accurate standoff weapons moving on to the scene will have cascading effects that fundamentally alter the structure of future conflicts. The most radical change to the war paradigm appears to be the distortion of time caused by advanced sensor technology, the rapid dissemination of information, and long-range PGM's. Increasingly, the strategy of choice in conventional warfare will be to decapitate the enemy with a single, well-aimed, strike. As this excerpt points out, in response units will have to become smaller. Similarly, as the lethality of these small units increases due to technological advances and greater freedom of action, they in turn become capable of realizing disproportionately large results in relation to their size. Long-range PGM's will threaten large concentrations of forces requiring that units either disperse or move into areas where detection becomes degraded. This has driven some to speculate that warfare will move into the cities where high-tech sensors are less effective. Increased interest in the art of deception may also gain renewed interest due to the fact that long-range

PGM's have effectively decoupled the historical link between range and accuracy.

Finally, along with the rise in PGM's an alternative model for force modernization needs to be briefly addressed. This alternative model can be found by continuously adapting existing systems in ways that completely transform the original concept of the platform. The evolution of the B-52 and its employment is an example of this trend along with the possible conversion of several SSBN's[62] from their original nuclear deterrence role to special operations platforms. Additionally, the incorporation of off-the-shelf technology allows organizations the opportunity to keep up with the pace of change and/or alter and redirect existing systems and weapons. This alternative path to force modernization is especially attractive to those who do not have the capital to pursue high dollar upgrades.

For those who do not have the luxury of wealth, more use will be made of strap-on technologies to upgrade and extend the life of existing systems. Information technologies able to link dissimilar systems together and provide enhanced, and decentralized, command and control also act as enablers for this type of force modernization.

---

[62] Nuclear-powered Ballistic Missile Submarine.

In combination, the proliferation of weapons and technology could lead to the development of very capable, state of the art, hybrid forces with fewer inhibitions that are able to challenge the premier militaries. The Eritrean Defense Force's hybrid response to naval operations during their thirty-year fight for independence provides a real-world glimpse of this concept in action.

In conclusion, the tactical technology trends section has examined the more tangible, at hand, trends in military affairs closely related to those addressed in the near-term RMA discussion. The purpose of doing so has been to add greater depth to the conflict in the information age framework by identifying those enhanced warfighting tools and tactics currently in place in the operating environment. In particular, these trends have focused attention on the consequences of establishing the primacy of precision and the low-investment strategies available in the absence of a RMA. In doing so an alternative framework of military affairs in the coming decades can be developed offering a hedged view of information age conflict.

F.   INTERPRETING THE EVOLUTIONARY FRAMEWORK

Although this chapter has analyzed the trends emerging in all three components of the chapter's framework, and does not dismiss the possibility of a full RMA in the early decades of the twenty-first century, the hedged view offered by the evolutionary framework may provide a more realistic vision of crisis, conflict, and war in the near-term future. Figure 4 is a graphical summary of the evolutionary view this chapter has developed superimposed on the chapter's three primary components.

Geostrategic Setting

- Crisis, conflict, and war are coming
- Geostrategic reordering
- Rapid pace of technological change
- War increasingly unconventional in nature

Revolution in Military Affairs

- Information-based RMA
- Revolutionary or evolutionary?
  - **RMA's 2 Lobes**

Near-term	Long-term
Technology	Operational & Organizational

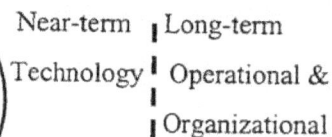

Will they come together?

- The high-technology trends
- The highly-sophisticated trends
- Asymmetrical/Asynchronous Strategies
- The conventional emphasis of the RMA enables the low-tech/highly sophisticated opponent

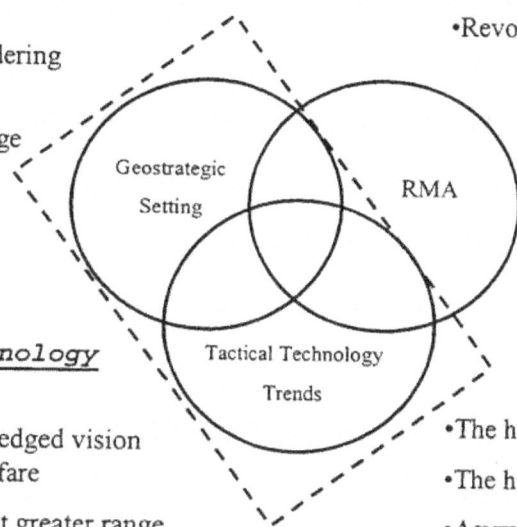

Tactical Technology Trends

- T3 trends offer a hedged vision of the future of warfare
- Greater precision at greater range
- Low-investment trends
- A blend of conventional and unconventional elements

Figure 4. The Evolution in Military Affairs (EMA)

The major themes developed in each section are briefly identified and summarized. The alternate evolutionary-centric interpretation this chapter implicitly develops can be found bounded by the rectangular portion of the figure. This view of crisis, conflict, and war is focused more on the evolutionary realities of warfare vice its revolutionary possibilities and may be a useful tool for understanding the future of MIW. The arguments contained in the EMA framework will be the ones used in the concluding chapter.

THIS PAGE INTENTIONALLY LEFT BLANK

IV. IMPLICATIONS FOR THE FUTURE

It was not the legions which crossed the Rubicon, but Caesar.

- Napoleon Bonaparte

With the primary surveys of the MIW concept and the trends in information age conflict completed, the final task that remains is to fuse the core arguments made in each of these main sections. This thesis will use three key areas derived from the mainbody to develop a composite picture of MIW's place in the information age.

A. STAYING POWER

One of the more obvious conclusions that can be drawn from the MIW analysis is that the irregular approach to naval warfare has been around a long time. The application of MIW is not a new phenomenon, nor has it recently come into existence in response to modern warfare or twentieth century improvements in technology. These facts support this theses primary argument that maritime irregular warfare is a fundamental part of naval warfare strategy. Although conventional naval warfare holds the premier position in naval affairs, MIW constitutes a less understood but equally important "other" tradition in naval affairs. Two complementary relationships found in the MIW analysis account for its historical staying power.

Sir Francis Drake's exploits in the Caribbean and later along the coasts of mainland Europe; Britain's decision to employ Q-ships against the German U-boat juggernaut during World War I; and the approach that the Italian 10th Light Flotilla took in countering the Allies conventional superiority in the Mediterranean during World War II all originated from one common trait: an unconventional mindset.

Throughout history the ability to think and act unconventionally has allowed MIW forces to identify enemy weaknesses and capitalize on opportunities by combining innovative, unorthodox operational techniques with the most current technologies. Unconstrained, MIW has had a powerful influence on naval affairs and succeeded in affecting the outcomes of conflict both at sea and on land. Drake's unique vision and unorthodox methods revolutionized sea power and his exploits had a lasting effect on British strategic thought in the late 1500's. In terms of numbers of German submarines sunk during World War I, the overall effectiveness of British Q-ships can be called into question. But, the consequences of this protracted special operation succeeded in shifting the overall balance of World War I and played a decisive role in the war's final outcome.

Finally, the Italian 10th Light Flotilla's unconventional mindset and approach is ultimately what enabled it to deploy a potent unconventional response to the Allies conventional superiority in the Mediterranean that is still the subject of intense study.

Another reason for MIW's longevity is its operational flexibility. Through the years MIW has come packaged in a variety of forms and offered a number of unique capabilities. Highlighting this point played an important role in determining which cases would be examined in the MIW typology. Additionally, maritime irregular warfare has proven its effectiveness across the spectrum of war and been utilized offensively and defensively for both protracted and short duration special operations. In addition to these more recognizable roles in conflict, the MIW approach has been equally effective below the military horizon by providing alternative avenues for intelligence gathering along with highly sophisticated entrepreneurial options. Far from the conventional image of irregular warfare as a fragile form of warfare easily countered by conventional doctrine, restricted in range, and inevitably the ad hoc strategy of a weaker opponent, MIW has shown operational dynamism and proven capable of persevering under extreme conditions while providing an array of diverse options.

The continual evolution and upgrade of MIW capabilities has been the key to its flexibility. As MIW continues to expand into every aspect of the naval environment, it creates additional opportunities and provides battlefield commanders with the ability to act unconventionally and rapidly adjust to changing situations. When combined with the right type of people afforded the freedom to think and act unconventionally, MIW has proven to offer a highly effective style of warfare with an impressive record of accomplishments to back it up.

Working in tandem, the unconventional mindset and MIW's inherent flexibility account for MIW's historical staying power. The elements identified in the emerging geostrategic setting discussion also fit nicely with these two tenets and point to MIW's continued longevity.

The first point to be made in the emerging geostrategic setting disscussion was that crisis, conflict, and war will continue to be a fundamental part of the near-term strategic landscape. Upon closer inspection two identifiable fault lines were addressed: 1) the geostrategic reordering, and 2) the rapid pace of technological change. Maritime irregular warfare has already proven to be a very capable complement to the trends emerging in these two categories. For starters, the simultaneous increase in the number of internal breakdowns and the rise of aggressive non-state threats are credited as fueling a potential geostrategic reordering. This translates into a likely increase in activity throughout the low-intensity spectrum and in other forms of conflict below the conventional threshold. Maritime irregular warfare has already been tapped in response to a similar environmental dynamic. For example, during Eritrea's thirty-year fight for independence from Ethiopia the EPLF's introduction of a hybrid high-speed gunboat enabled the employment a very successful MIW strategy against the Ethiopian Armed Forces. In Sri Lanka the LTTE is currently using a very effective MIW strategy in the northern part of the island to maintain control over strategically important locations along the Jaffna Peninsula. And, during times of relative peace, MIW concepts continue to be employed in conjunction with maritime piracy, and the maritime components of the drug trade.

In each of these cases an aggressive non-state actor has pursued and profited from the advantages of an MIW strategy. In the first case MIW was part of an overall strategy that eventually led to the creation of the state of Eritrea. In the second case, while the war between the LTTE and Sri Lankan government still continues, few will deny that the LTTE is currently the most dangerous terrorist-insurgent group in the world. The development of an effective MIW denial strategy has effectively allowed the LTTE to maintain intermittent control over strategic points along the Jaffna Peninsula in the face of a much larger conventionally equipped opponent. And in the last example, the sophisticated entrepreneurial forms of MIW have proven to be operationally robust in the face of conventional counter measures and have yet to be effectively suppressed. These are just a few examples but they all suggest that as the elements identified in the geostrategic reordering begin to take shape, MIW will continue to be called upon globally.

The rapid pace of technological change was the other area of focus contained within the emerging geostrategic setting. While independent IW appears to be evolving into its own separate form of warfare, MIW will be incorporated into the integrated aspects of IW that involve improving situational awareness. In addition to MIW maintaining the collateral ability to clarify the battlefield through intelligence collection, one emerging trend in this arena seems clear, maritime irregular warfare forces will no longer be allowed to conduct unsupervised operations.

In large-scale engagements the increasingly integrated nature of conventional warfare and its rapid acceleration in operational tempo will force MIW forces to become apart of the commanders common operational picture. Increasingly, battlefield commanders will demand improved monitoring of MIW forces while in the field. This desire for improved tracking and monitoring of MIW forces will also extend down to smaller-scale confrontations in which MIW is the focus of effort. As the spread of sophisticated information technologies along with the advanced information architecture linking these systems together becomes readily available, MIW forces will increasingly become part of the integrated aspects of IW emerging in the geostrategic setting.

The other, non-technical, side of technological change that affects the future of MIW involves the adoption of cutting edge technologies. Maritime irregular warfare has a history of staying on the cusp of cutting edge technology and tactical innovation. During World War II PT boats were renowned for their speed and maneuverability. And in the Mediterranean the 10th Light Flotilla developed a submarine entry/exit method that allowed them to launch and recover *Maiale's* while remaining submerged, greatly reducing the risk of detection. When MIW forces have not been able to produce state-of-the-art hardware inhouse, they have always found other innovative ways to benefit from the advantages of the latest leading technologies. This alternative path to

increased capability has led to the creation of some very
capable hybrid MIW forces. The information age conflict
analysis suggests that it is forces displaying these traits
that will pose the greatest challenge to less dynamic
conventionally oriented militaries.

A review of MIW's record reveals that technological
change has never equated to obsolescence from the MIW
perspective. Maritime irregular warfare forces have proven
to be quite resilient and comfortable with the pace of
technological change, and have consistently used cutting
edge technology to gain an advantage over the enemy and stay
unpredictable.

B. HIGH-LEVERAGE FORCES

Another area of convergence found between the MIW
analysis and the trends emerging in crisis, conflict, and
war concerns the enduring requirement for high-leverage
forces. These types of forces can usually be characterized
by small investments in men and materiel relative to the
costs of manning and equipping larger formations for
conventionally oriented operations. In addition, the
signature of any high-leverage force is the ability to yield
disproportionately large results in relation to its size.
One theme that runs throughout the information age conflict

framework is that in the near-term future there will be expanding opportunities for forces displaying these traits.

Historically speaking, MIW elements have always fit the definition of a high-leverage force. The cases highlighted in the MIW typology implicitly point out this side of the maritime irregular warfare concept. Sir Francis Drake's refinement of the classical maritime raiding strategy easily qualifies as an example of a high-leverage force. His unique vision and unorthodox methods revolutionized sea power and his exploits had a lasting effect on British strategic thought. In this instance the costs, in terms of men and materiel, of outfitting naval guerrillas for maritime raiding operations were minor compared to the costs of assembling the men and materiel necessary for much larger fleet actions. One defining feature of all MIW forces has been their comparatively small size and low cost, relative to the manning and materiel requirements necessary for fielding conventional forces of the day. This also helps partially explain maritime irregular warfare's universal attractiveness, especially to aggressive actors with limited resources.

The same kind of logical cost-benefit analysis can be applied to the MIW cases cited during World War I. Here, Britain's employment of Q-ships easily passes both conditions necessary for consideration as a high-leverage force. Meanwhile, the blocking of Zeebrugge operation, while falling short of its intended objective, did possess the potential to shift the overall naval balance of the war with a small investment in men and materiel.

Both World War II cases cited stand as classic examples of very capable and successful high-leverage MIW forces in action.[63] In the Pacific campaign the PT boats high-leverage advantage originally grew out of the necessity to blunt the Imperial Japanese Navy's conventional superiority with a low-cost, expendable response. Later, U.S. "mosquito boats" solidified their position in the Pacific campaign by being operationally flexible and by evolving and adapting over the course of the war. But by far the best example of a high-leverage MIW force during World War II comes out of the Mediterranean Theater. For three years *Decima Mas/Mariassalto* relentlessly engaged in unconventional MIW operations against the Allies. During that time it came to

---

[63] It should also be pointed out that it is roughly during this period that MIW actions became increasingly labor intensive. Although the quantities of men and materiel remained relatively small, because of the rising complexity of MIW operations even small loses could be critical given the time needed to train new MIW personnel and ready new MIW weaponry. This fact may take on even greater emphasis in the near-term future as more advanced technologies and systems make their way on to the battlefield.

epitomize the modern high-leverage MIW force and embody the traits accounting for MIW's historical staying power. Although the Royal Italian Navy ended its offensive role in 1943 by surrendering to the Allies, while operational *Decima Mas'* maritime irregular warfare strategy succeeded in challenging the Allies naval supremacy in the Mediterranean.

The presence of high-leverage forces has been one of warfare's constants in the years following World War II as well. Maritime irregular warfare has successfully answered that calling in such places as the Korean Peninsula, the coast of Eritrea, the Falkland Islands, and Sri Lanka to recognize just a few contemporary examples. Modern-day pirates and the maritime components of the drug trade have also tapped into MIW's low-cost, high yield advantage and the analysis of information age conflict suggests that the need and opportunities for these types of forces will continue unabated into the near-term future.

The tactical technology trends disscussion went the furthest in actually exploring and explaining the future opportunities for high-leverage forces. A brief summary sheds light on some of the emerging warfighting trends that will enable MIW forces to maintain their high-leverage tradition.

For maritime irregular warfare to survive on the future battlefield MIW forces will first have to come to terms with, and capitalize on three technology driven variables: precision, range, and time. In the T3 disscussion the global push towards establishing the primacy of precision, the ability to strike targets at greater range, and the ensuing increase in operational tempo were credited as the force behind units becoming smaller, more mobile, and dispersed on the future battlefield. This part of the high-leverage equation may not be that difficult for MIW to achieve. In a certain sense MIW has always fit this mold. Maritime irregular warfare has shown itself to be predisposed to using advanced technology in order to gain an advantage, and MIW forces have always been packaged in small mobile units. The key for MIW in this area may be understanding this historical dynamic and incorporating the right technologies and systems that allow MIW to stay operationally dynamic.

The second area that MIW will have to master in order to maintain its high-leverage label involves the trends associated with the changing nature of command. In order to compensate for the time compression on the battlefield, decentralized tactical command and greater centralized strategic control will be needed so that MIW units can react quickly to rapidly changing situations while remaining connected. Devolving greater freedom of action to subordinate units can only be operationalized by reducing the layers of command and control, and improving information avenues. By taking these steps towards more streamlined and efficient command and control structures the lethality of the small unit increases and MIW's high-leverage advantage remains secure.

It should once again be stressed that the concepts described in this section will not reside solely in the domain of the premier militaries. Whether developed inhouse or arrived at by combining and adapting dissimilar systems they will be available to everyone. Applied by an opponent capable of thinking and acting unconventionally, high-leverage MIW forces operating with an asymmetric/asynchronous strategy will pose a real threat to a less dynamic or conventionally oriented opponent.

C.   INTEGRATED AND INDEPENDENT MARITIME IRREGULAR WARFARE

In the near-term future when MIW is tasked to provide unorthodox options for sea control it will be provided either as an integrated part of a much larger plan, or independently as the sole means of achieving strategic objectives. Historically, all MIW operations have either been integrated or independent, making this distinction is not necessarily new. For example, during World War II PT boats were an integrated part of the U.S. Pacific campaign strategy. As the war progressed the operational flexibility of the PT force allowed it to remain an integral part of the island hoping strategy. Similarly, in the Mediterranean the 10th Light Flotilla was originally a minor unit integrated into the war plans of the conventionally oriented Royal Italian Navy. As the Allies summarily reduced the more conventional components of the RMI, the 10th Light Flotilla transitioned into the primary offensive arm within the Italian Navy. In the Pacific campaign MIW forces played a valuable supporting role in the conventionally driven war plan, while in the Mediterranean the 10th Light Flotilla was forced to slowly grow out of its supporting role as conventional RMI forces were defeated. The same cooperative relationship that existed between regular and irregular warfare during this period can be found in many of the conflicts that have followed the Second World War. In each case, MIW has provided unique capabilities that complemented, enabled, and enhanced conventional forces. For integrated MIW operations to be successful MIW forces have historically relied upon, and maintained, a strong connection with the conventional fleet in order to ensure the proper synchronization and unity of effort.

In the near-term future integrated operations will'
remain a key role for MIW forces that operate in tandem with
a conventional component. By clarifying the battlefield for
conventional commanders through intelligence gathering
operations and simplifying the battlefield by eliminating
critical targets linked to the conventional campaign, MIW
will continue to provide a vital force multiplier that
conventional forces can not afford to dismiss. Additionally,
by working closely with regular naval forces, the irregular
approach to naval warfare becomes more widely accepted as
MIW's capabilities are put on display, meanwhile
opportunities for employment and additional capabilities
gained through joint operations with the conventional
battlefleet expand.

Aided by improved information systems that will enable
MIW units to be tied into the conventional campaign, and the
increasing lethality of the small unit, highly mobile MIW
forces will continue to provide unconventional solutions to
complex military problems during conventional campaigns. The
rationale behind MIW's historical staying power and its
high-leverage advantage will help facilitate MIW's place on
the conventional and unconventional battlefields of the
future. In the premier navies that view naval affairs
primarily through a conventional perspective, MIW forces

will be required to provide critical, complementary niche capabilities and continuously upgrade and adjust to meet the needs of the fleet. By doing so, the synergy achieved by synchronizing regular and irregular naval warfare will allow strategic objectives to be attained faster, and with fewer costs associated with warfare.

Not every group waging war on the sea has the luxury of being able to field conventional and unconventional forces at the same time, nor are they required to when backed by a sound independent MIW strategy.[64] Independent operations imply that MIW is the primary means of achieving naval objectives, not just an adjunct in a conventional naval campaign. In this context MIW can suspend the bonds that hold it in a supporting role to regular naval warfare, thus allowing MIW operations to become the focus of effort. Where resources are stretched thin, independent MIW has proven to be an effective alternative and counter to conventional naval warfare by allowing all combat power available to be employed in the most effective way possible. For instance,

---

[64] The RMA analysis suggests that the greatest threat to forces relying on high-tech advances for conventional superiority will most likely come from an opponent employing low-technology tools and a highly sophisticated asymmetrical/asynchronous strategy to circumvent, blind, or nullify a high-tech advantage. Maritime irregular warfare is particularly well equipped to serve in that function.

during Eritrea's fight for independence a severe lack of resources restricted the EPLF from employing conventional assets. Therefore, they turned to a low investment, high yield independent MIW strategy that proved to be an effective answer to the conventional Ethiopian Navy. The quality of the conventional opponent can also be a deciding factor in the turn towards independent MIW. One of reasons behind the LTTE's independent MIW strategy is that conventional assets would be easier for the SLN to target and destroy. In both of these examples independent maritime irregular warfare in effect became the naval strategy.

The conflict in the information age analysis suggests that, as fighting units become smaller, swifter, and more lethal in the near-term future, the ability of MIW to act independently in pursuit of strategic objectives will increase. The lessons learned from past successes and the trends identified in the EMA will allow independent MIW operations to challenge and/or negate conventional naval operations. When MIW's doctrinal flexibility and diverse range of action are added to this mix, independent MIW operations have the potential to pose a direct threat to conventional opponents. Historically, MIW has proven to be the most operationally dynamic when placed in a leading role and unconstrained by having to work within a conventional system. Aided by the trends emerging in information age conflict, independent MIW strategies will increasingly become an impending part of the naval war paradigm.

Regardless of whether the operations are integrated or independent the findings of this thesis suggest that when MIW is brought into action in the near-term future it will be strategically employed in two basic forms.[65] In the first form, a single MIW operation may be initiated with the intention of yielding immediate results, as in a *coup de main*. An alternative method that also seems to be gaining strength involves mounting a MIW campaign. This would take the form of a series of interrelated missions in which the cumulative effects had a crippling effect on the enemy.

1. Decisive Action

Although the World War I examples of MIW were not resounding successes, the style and approach they introduced may actually hold the key to MIW's future, especially when the trends in information age conflict are factored in. As envisioned the blocking of Zeebrugge was designed to take

---

[65] Maritime irregular warfare can perform a variety of tasks and provide numerous capabilities. This theses primary focus is on the strategic application of MIW in the information age. The two basic forms identified here will not cover *all* the possible uses of MIW in the future, but rather seek to distinguish the general direction and strategic character of future MIW operations.

94

the German U-boats stationed at Bruges out of war with a single, swift, decisive stroke. While this MIW operation was launched with the intention of delivering immediate strategic results by shifting the naval balance, it was still an integrated part of a much larger on going war. Although this operation did yield some short-term success, the originally desired long-term results were not achieved for a number of reasons cited in the MIW typology.

At the core, the blocking of Zeebrugge was planned as a decisive MIW action against a fixed target on land. This is the critical point to take away from this short duration MIW operation.

On the near-term battlefield MIW units will continue to engage in *coup de main* style decisive actions similar in design to the one attempted at Zeebrugge. A review of the trends emerging in information age conflict and the evolution of the MIW concept suggest that in the near-term future these types of operations will most likely be conducted against fixed targets on land. The increasingly destructive power of the small unit suggests that this type of raiding will become more effective in the future.

The high-technology trends identified in the RMA disscussion suggest that in the near-term future the initial period may in effect be the only period of future warfare.

This analysis further indicates that the rapid pace of technological change is ushering in a new era of increased operational tempo. Therefore, in order for MIW forces to maintain the element of surprise, military actions will have to become short, sharp, and decisive.[66] These kinds of sudden, crippling blows will not be delivered against dispersed, mobile targets, but against critical targets that are fixed, and within close proximity to the littorals.

2. The MIW Campaign

The Q-ship campaign undertaken by Britain during World War I may also provide valuable clues to MIW's future when the trends identified in information age conflict and the evolution of MIW are combined. The British Q-ship campaign was launched in response to effective U-boat operations slowly paralyzing British war production and sea communications during World War I. While the tangible results of the Q-ship campaign were modest at best, the consequences of this protracted maritime special operation forced Germany to radically alter its submarine doctrine, substantially reducing U-boat effectiveness on patrol. In

---

[66] Decisive action may also come in alternative forms in the near-term future. For instance, the Information Age Conflict analysis suggested that winning by mass disruption and paralysis may increasingly become the strategy of choice against technology dependent opponents.

addition, fear of Q-ships led to sinkings without warning, which had the unintended effect of provoking neutrals into entering the war against Germany.

At its core, the Q-ship campaign represented a protracted maritime irregular warfare operation against highly mobile targets at sea. This is the critical conclusion to draw from this example and something that, again, will be reenergized by technology trends.

A review of the evolution of MIW and the trends emerging in information age conflict suggest that in the near-term future MIW forces will increasingly engage in protracted campaigns similar in character to British Q-ship operations during World War I. Additionally, these campaigns appear to be the most likely in conflicts below the conventional threshold as witnessed in the Eritrean and Sri Lankan examples.

The primary enabler for the MIW campaign on the near-term battlefield will be the advances accrued from improved command and control. The MIW campaign differs from decisive action not only in terms of the time horizon but also in the measures of effectiveness used to define success or failure. With a single *coup de main*, the immediate military result following the mission is what signifies success or failure. In a campaign the process is subtler as it is the cumulative effect of the missions that become more important. As units become smaller, more mobile, and dispersed upon the battlefield in order to avoid being decapitated by a single decisive action, MIW will need to develop the ability to find and destroy these hard to find targets. The move towards decentralized tactical command with greater centralized control and the technological advances leading towards a more transparent battlefield and improved situational awareness will combine to enable MIW forces to better succeed in campaigns similar to the one undertaken by Q-ships during World War I.

In conclusion, maritime irregular warfare will be an active element of future conflicts. When the arguments supporting MIW's staying power and high-leverage advantage are combined with the primary enablers driving MIW's move toward decisive actions and the MIW campaign, a powerful image of maritime irregular warfare in the near-term future begins to emerge. By combining the evolution of MIW with the emerging trends in crisis, conflict, and war this thesis has developed a picture that indicates MIW may be gaining momentum in naval affairs. In addition to putting the irregular side of naval warfare into perspective and offering a vision of MIW's future, it is hoped that the approach and broader themes developed throughout this thesis will spark increased interest in, and discussion of, the future of maritime irregular warfare.

THIS PAGE INTENTIONALLY LEFT BLANK

LIST OF REFERENCES

Alexander, B., *The Future of Warfare*, New York NY: W.W. Norton & Company, 1995.

Army After Next (AAN) Annual Report FY1998, 1998.

Army Vision 2010, 1996.
[http://www.army.mil/2010/default.htm].

Arquilla, J. (Ed.), *From Troy to Entebbe: Special Operations in Ancient and Modern Times*, Lanham MD: University Press of America, 1996.

Arquilla, J. & Ronfeldt, D., *In Athena's Camp: Preparing for Conflict in the Information Age*, Santa Monica CA: RAND, 1997.

Bermudez, J., *DPRK Seaborne Infiltration Operations: June-December 1998*,
[http://www.nyu.edu/globalbeat/asia/bermudez010799.html].

Clapham, C. (Ed.), *African Guerrillas*, Indiana University Press, 1998.

Commander Naval Special Warfare Group One: *The Plan*, 2000.

Connell, D., *Against All Odds: A Chronicle of the Eritrean Revolution*, Red Sea Press, 1993.

DEPARTMENT OF THE NAVY, *Naval Doctrine Publication 1: Naval Warfare*, Washington DC, 1994.

Forward...from the Sea (1994), Basic Documents in National Security: A Source Book for Studies in United States Military Strategy, Monterey CA, 1996.

Friedman, G. & Friedman, M., *The Future of War: Power, Technology and American World Dominance in the Twenty-First Century*, New York NY: Crown Publishers, 1996.

...From the Sea (1992), Basic Documents in National Security: A Source Book for Studies in United States Military Strategy, Monterey CA, 1996.

Global Reach, Global Power (1992), Basic Documents in National Security: A Source Book for Studies in United States Military Strategy, Monterey CA, 1996.

Gunaratna, R., *Sri Lanka's Ethnic Crisis and National Security*, Colombo: South Asian Network on Conflict Research, 1998.

Henderson, B., *The Great War Between Athens and Sparta*, Arno Press Inc., 1973.

Hough, R., *The Great War at Sea 1914-1918*, Oxford University Press, 1983.

Hughes, W., *Fleet Tactics and Coastal Combat*, Naval Institute Press, 2000.

Jane's Intelligence Review, *The Tanker War*, Jane's Information Group Limited, 1 May 1992.

Joint Pub 1-02, *Department of Defense Dictionary of Military and Associated Terms*, 1989.

Kaplan, R., *The Coming Anarchy*, The Atlantic Monthly, February, 1994.

Kemp, P., *Underwater Warriors*, Annapolis MD: The Naval Institute Press, 1996.

McRaven, W., *Spec Ops: Case Studies in Special Operations Warfare: Theory and Practice*, Novato CA: Presidio Press, 1995.

Naval Special Warfare Strategic Plan 2000, 2000.

Nelson, C., *Hunters in the Shallows: A History of the PT Boat*, Brassey's Books, 1998.

Operational Maneuver from the Sea, 1996. [http://www.dtic.mil/jv2010/usmc/omfts.pdf].

Pfaltzgraff, R. & Shultz, R. (Ed.), *War in the Information Age: New Challenges for U.S. Security*, Dulles VA: Brassey's Books, 1997.

Sadkovich, J., *The Italian Navy in World War II*, Greenwood Press, 1994.

Scales, R., *Future Warfare: Anthology*, Carlisle Barracks PA: U.S. Army War College, 1999.

Sharpe, R. (Ed.), *Jane's Fighting Ships: 1999-2000*, Jane's Information Group Inc, 1999.

Training and Doctrine Command (TRADOC), *Pam 525-5*, 1994, [http://www-tradoc.army.mil/tpubs/pams/p525-5.htm].

Urban Warrior Conceptual Experimental Framework, Version 1-5, 1998.

Van Creveld, M., *The Transformation of War*, New York NY: The Free Press, 1991.

White, W., *They Were Expendable: American Torpedo Boat Squadron in the U.S. Retreat from the Philippines*, Naval Institute Press, 1998.

THIS PAGE INTENTIONALLY LEFT BLANK

INITIAL DISTRIBUTION LIST

1. Defense Technical Information Center. 2
   8725 John J. Kingman Rd. Ste 0944
   Fort Belvoir, VA 22060-6218

2. Dudley Knox Library. 2
   Naval Postgraduate School
   411 Dyer Rd.
   Monterey, CA 93943-5101

3. Professor Gordon H. McCormick. 1
   Chairman, Special Operations Academic Group
   (Code CC/Mc)
   Naval Postgraduate School
   Monterey, CA 93943-5000

4. Professor John Arquilla. 1
   (Code CC/AR)
   Naval Postgraduate School
   Monterey, CA 93943

5. RADM Eric T. Olson. 1
   Commander
   Naval Special Warfare Command
   NAB Coronado
   San Diego, CA 92155

6. CAPT John McTighe. 1
   Commander
   Naval Special Warfare Development Group
   1636 Regulus Ave.
   Virginia Beach, VA 23461

7. Jennifer Duncan. 3
   Special Operations Academic Group
   Code (CC/Jd)
   Naval Postgraduate School
   Monterey, CA 93943-5000

8. Library. 1
   Army War College
   Carlisle Barracks, PA 17013

9.   Library. .1
     Naval War College
     Newport, RI 02840

10. Department of Military Strategy. 1
     National War College (NWMS)
     Ft. Leslie J. McNair
     Washington, DC 20319-6111

11. US Army Command and General Staff College. 1
     Attn: Library
     Ft. Leavenworth, KS 66027-6900

12. Library. .1
     Air War College
     Maxwell AFB, AL 36112-6428

13. US Military Academy. 1
     Attn: Library
     West Point, NY 10996

14. US Naval Academy. 1
     Attn: Library
     Annapolis, MD 21412

15. Maraquat Memorial Library. 1
     US Army John F. Kennedy Special Warfare Center
     Rm. C287, Bldg 3915
     Ft. Bragg, NC 28307-5000

16. Commander. 1
     Naval Special Warfare Group One
     NAB Coronado
     San Diego, CA 92155

17. Commanding Officer 1
     Seal Team Five
     2348 Trident Way
     San Diego, CA 92155-5597

18. US Special Operations Command. 1
     Attn: Command Historian
     McDill AFB, FL 33608-6001

19. BGen R.H. Sutton. 1
     8461 Highway 19 East
     Roan Mountain, TN 37687

20.	LT W.R. Sutton. 1
	Seal Team Five
	2348 Trident Way
	San Diego, CA 92155-5597